Humor, Psyche, and Society
A Socio-Semiotic Analysis

Arthur Asa Berger
San Francisco State University

Series in Anthropology

VERNON PRESS

www.vernonpress.com

In the Americas:
Vernon Press
1000 N West Street,
Suite 1200, Wilmington,
Delaware 19801
United States

In the rest of the world:
Vernon Press
C/Sancti Espiritu 17,
Malaga, 29006
Spain

Series in Anthropology

Library of Congress Control Number: 2020936549

ISBN: 978-1-64889-096-3

Also available: 978-1-62273-808-3 [Hardback]; 978-1-64889-045-1 [PDF, E-Book]

Illustrated by the Author

"How Jokes Work: Seven Humor Theorists in Search of a Joke" was published in Arie Sover, Ed. *The Languages of Humor: Verbal, Visual, and Physical Humor,* Bloomsbury Academic, 2018, and is reprinted with permission.
"How Humor Heals", 2005, was published in *European Journal of Psychology,* and is reprinted with permission.
"Laugh and the World Laughs with You: Global Humor", 2007, was published in *Global Media Journal,* and is reprinted with permission.
"Little Britain: An American Perspective" was published in Sharon Lockyear, Ed., Reading Little Britain, 2010, I.B. Taurus/Bloomsbury and is reprinted with permission.
"Mediated Myth or *Frasier's* "The Good Son", was published in A. A. Berger, *The Agent in the Agency,* 2003, Hampton Press, and is reprinted with permission.
"Anatomy of the Joke", was published in *Journal of Communication* 2006, Oxford University Press, and is reprinted with permission.
An earlier version of "I Laughed and Lasted" was published as "I Laughed Last, and I Lasted, But I Took Some Blows Along the Way", in *Studies in American Humor,* Vol. 13, 2005-2009, 87-98, and is used by permission of The Pennsylvania State University Press.

Contents

Table of Figures

Table of Tables

Preface
by
Arie Sover

Humor has a language of its own. Verbal humor is attached to the normative language, reflecting our rational ordinary thinking. At some point, humor decides to turn on a path of its own, abandons the expected pattern of thought created at the beginning of the story (or joke), and turns to new directions. Common routine language is not the way of humor.

Humor tends to play with exceptional patterns of thinking, which cause us pleasure and satisfaction when we manage to understand the extraordinary cognitive path, and actually the language of humor. The brain acts as a nerve network that organizes itself; a system that classifies the new information it receives into patterns it recognizes. If this system cannot embed information into an existing pattern, it creates a new pattern. In this self-organizing information system, an idea can seem completely logical after application, but it is difficult to be predicted in advance. In this way, humor is created (de Bono, 1994, 28-29).

The language of humor is based on the normative language, but it is much richer. The language of humor, using a cognitive process, knows how to connect words and phrases that do not relate in the normative language. By doing so, humor creates a whole new language of its own. The uniqueness of the language of humor is its ability to regenerate itself over and over again. As opposed to the normative language, which usually has constant basic patterns, the language of humor has a surprising ability to modify itself within a moment. Comparing normative language with humor language, we see two conflicting cognitive behaviors of the brain. In normative language, the brain operates within rational, well-organized patterns, rejecting everything that is not compatible with these patterns. In humor language, the brain operates in contrast with normative activity, allowing itself to break the rules of the game and chooses ways in which impossible cognitive and intellectual connections become possible, within the moment in which humor is created.

Humor language is based on three levels: verbal, psychological and cultural. On the **verbal level,** there is the ability of the joke's creator or receiver to interpret its complexity and reach the desired solution. It is similar to the intellectual effort of solving a crossword puzzle or understanding a caricature. On the **psychological level,** we refer to the personality traits of the one who receives and responses to a joke. The response to a joke or a humor situation depends on other factors, such as the mental or physical condition during absorption, and the attitude, positive or negative, to the content of the joke. People perceive humor positively when the source of humor is something that they identify with. The more humor is perceived as positive for them, the more positive is the appreciation of this humor (Zillmann & Cantor, 1972). Responds to humor can sometimes result in big laughter or in a little smile. Therefore, in order to analyze humorous situations, we have to distinguish and separate between laughter, which is the response to humor, and humor itself, which activates laughter (Attardo, 2003). Jokes and humor situations are **culturally based**. The content of the joke refers to the cultural world of the joke's target audience. The assumption is that there are shared cultural similarities and common ground between the joke's creator and the target audience. Thanks to this common ground, the response will be laughter (Gervais, M., & Wilson, D. 2005, Raskin 1985). Indicating laughter as a response, we also classify smiling in the same category, since smile is also in the hierarchy of responses for comic, humorous, verbal, visual or other situations.

Arthur Asa Berger goes deeper into these three aspects of humor: the structure of humor, humor and the psyche, and humor and society. He refers to laughter as a tool of criticism that is based on true expression of opinion or as he calls it "A free weapon in people's hands." Arthur is a prolific academic researcher on various areas of knowledge, one of which is humor research. He has written many articles and a number of books on humor such as *Li'l Abner: A Study in American Satire* (1970), *The Comic-Stripped American* (1974), *Anatomy of the Joke* (1976), *An Anatomy of Humor* (1993), *Blind Men and Elephants: Perspectives on Humor* (1995), *The Art of Comedy Writing* (1997), *Jewish Jesters* (2001), and *The Genius of the Jewish Joke* (2005).

This new book is a collection of important studies written by the author and in addition, it includes new chapters that all together enrich the reader's knowledge on the study of humor and laughter. One of his humor research focuses is analyzing the techniques of jokes, from which he conceived his own structural and semiotic theory or typology. This typology helps us analyze verbal and physical humor and is found in many of his chapters, his **"45 techniques of humor."**

Addressing the semiotics of verbal humor, the author does not forget to mention the inventor of semiotics F. de Saussure which - even if not intended to - is also the 'forefather' of verbal humor studies. Many new humor researchers don't mention Saussure as such and are satisfied to refer in their studies to new semioticians. Other chapters in the book deal with important aspects of humor research such as humor and health, Jewish humor and Ethnic humor.

One of the author's privileges is that one of his chapters focuses on his contribution to humor not only as a scholar but also as an artist who produces humorous text. For those who are acquainted with his humor research, it is nice and refreshing to meet another and quite surprising aspect of the author dealing with humor. The same goes with his last chapter *I Laughed Last, and I Lasted, (But I Took Some Blows Along the Way")*, *My Scholarly Work on Humor.* The chapter begins that way "I see myself as essentially a humorist who did his gigs in universities, not comedy clubs. This has caused problems for me with some academicians who take themselves seriously and with many of my students, who didn't know how to take me" and another quote "Being Jewish I am (it almost comes naturally) like many Jews, a Jewish humorist". Is this book a conclusion of the work of Arthur Asa Berger as a humor scholar who has contributed so much to humor research? I hope not. I strongly recommend this book as an important contribution to those who seek knowledge about humor and laughter as one of the most important human phenomena.

References

Attardo S. (2003). (Editorial) The Pragmatics of Humor, *Journal of Pragmatics*, 35. 1287-1294.

de Bono, A. (1994). *Lamed Et Yaldecha Lachshov* [Teach your children how to think]. Jerusalem: Branco Weiss Institute.

Gervais, M., Wilson, D. (2005). The Evolution and Functions of Laughter and Humor: A Synthetic Approach. *Quarterly Review of Biology*, 80(4), 395 - 430.

Gibbs, R. W. (1994). The Poetics of Mind. Cambridge: Cambridge University Press.

Raskin, V. (1985). *Semantic Mechanism of Humor.* Boston, MA: Dordfecht.

Zillmann, D., Cantor. (1972). "Directionality of transitory dominance as a communication variable affecting humor appreciation". *Journal of Personality and Social Psychology* 24: 191–198.

Laughter liberates not only from external censorship but first of all from the great interior censor; it liberates from the fear that has developed in man during thousands of years: fear of the sacred, of prohibitions, of power. It unveils the material bodily principle in its true meaning. Laughter opened men's eyes on that which is new, on the future. This is why it not only permitted the expression of an antifeudal, popular truth; it helped uncover this truth and give it an internal form. And this form was achieved and defended during thousands of years in its very depths and in its popular-festive images. Laughter showed the world anew in its gayest and most sober aspects. Its external privileges are intimately linked with interior forces; they are a recognition of the rights of these forces. This is why laughter could never become an instrument to oppress and blind the people. It always remained a free weapon in their hands.

As opposed to laughter, medieval seriousness was infused with elements of fear, weakness, humility, submission, falsehood, hypocrisy, or on the other hand, with violence, intimidation, threats, prohibitions. As a spokesman of power, seriousness terrorized, demanded and forbade... Distrust of the serious tone and confidence in the truth of laughter had a spontaneous, elemental character. It was understood that fear never lurks behind laughter...and that hypocrisy and lies never laugh but wear a serious mask. Laughter created no dogmas and could not become authoritarian; it did not convey fear but a feeling of strength. It was linked with the procreating act, with birth, renewal, fertility, abundance. Laughter was also related to food and drink and the people's earthy immortality, and finally, it was related to the future of things to come and was to clear the way for them.

Mikhail Bakhtin, *Rabelais and His World*: 1984:94-95

Introduction

This book reprints a number of my articles and chapters from books (some edited by other scholars) on various aspects of humor that I've written over the years. They appeared in some books and journals in the United States and other countries, and on Internet sites. A number of these articles involve Jewish humor, the subject of two of my books: *The Genius of the Jewish Joke* and *Jewish Jesters*. The chapters in *Humor, Psyche and Society* cover, broadly speaking, semiotic/structural, socio-political and psychoanalytic approaches to humor and reflect my approach to this fascinating and enigmatic subject. It also has some recent writings on humor.

The charts showing the 45 techniques of humor that I discuss in my article, "Anatomy of the Joke," appeared in the summer, 1976 issue of the *Journal of Communication*. It is very short and is the second chapter in this book. I used these techniques in my book, *An Anatomy of Humor* and many other articles and books I have written on humor and they are used in the chapters in this book where they play an important role in the analyses. I've also made some editorial changes to avoid repeating material discussed in several of the articles, but there is, you might expect, a certain amount of redundancy in the book. But not enough, I hope, to be bothersome.

The most commonly used justification for publishing a collection of previously published work is that doing so enables people interested in one's work to find this material available in one book. That is, collections of articles and chapters from books such as this save people interested in my work on humor a great deal of time and labor hunting down the material in books and journals. That is, books like this one are very convenient. They also serve to introduce my work to people interested in humor.

An important question to ask now is how is this book on humor different from other books on humor? My answer is that this book brings together my work that focuses upon three aspects of humor: the semiotics of humor, humor and the psyche, and humor and society. That's why the book is called *Humor, Psyche, and Society.* Informing the book is my focus on the structural/semiotic components of humor, as elaborated in my discovery of the 45 techniques of humor, elicited from a long content-analysis I made of humor many years ago. The techniques are shown below:

Table 0.1. Techniques of Humor by Category

LANGUAGE	LOGIC	IDENTITY	ACTION
Allusion	Absurdity	Before/After	Chase
Bombast	Accident	Burlesque	Slapstick
Definition	Analogy	Caricature	Speed
Exaggeration	Catalogue	Eccentricity	
Facetiousness	Coincidence	Embarrassment	
Insults	Comparison	Exposure	
Infantilism	Disappointment	Grotesque	
Irony	Ignorance	Imitation	
Literalness	Mistakes	Impersonation	
Misunderstanding	Repetition	Mimicry	
Puns/Wordplay	Reversal	Parody	
Repartee	Rigidity	Scale	
Ridicule	Theme/Variation	Stereotype	
Sarcasm	Unmasking		
Satire			

Techniques of Humor According to Category

When I found these techniques, I didn't realize that they could be fit into categories but eventually decided there were four categories of humor: humor involving language, humor involving logic, humor involving identity and humor involving action. These techniques can be put into alphabetical form and numbered, as shown in the chart that follows. This enumerated list enables us to deconstruct humorous texts with a degree of specificity which, I suggest, other approaches to humor do not allow.

Table 0.2. Techniques of Humor in Alphabetical Order

1. Absurdity	16. Embarrassment	31. Parody
2. Accident	17. Exaggeration	32. Puns
3. Allusion	18. Exposure	33. Repartee
4. Analogy	19. Facetiousness	34. Repetition
5. Before/After	20. Grotesque	35. Reversal
6. Bombast	21. Ignorance	36. Ridicule
7. Burlesque	22. Imitation	37. Rigidity
8. Caricature	23. Impersonation	38. Sarcasm

9. Catalogue	24. Infantilism	39. Satire
10. Chase Scene	25. Insults	40. Scale, Size
11. Coincidence	26. Irony	41. Slapstick
12. Comparison	27. Literalness	42. Speed
13. Definition	28. Mimicry	43. Stereotypes
14. Disappointment	29. Mistakes	44. Theme and Variation.
15. Eccentricity	30. Misunderstanding	45. Unmasking

Techniques Numbered and in Alphabetical Order

In a review of my book *The Art of Comedy Writing*, which appeared in *Humor: The International Journal of Humor Research* (*Humor, 12-1*, 1999:96, 97), the distinguished humor scholar Don L.F. Nilsen, writes:

> For the work that I am presently doing involving humor in British, American, and Irish literature, Arthur Asa Berger has provided a very insightful and useful methodology for analyzing and creating humorous discourse in his *The Art of Comedy Writing*. For me, his model is as powerful as such other discourse models as "Script Model Grammar," by Raskin and others, "Conversational Implicatures," by Grice and others, "Conversational Analysis," by Tannen and others, "Genre and Archetype Theory," by Frye, White, and others, "Signification Theory," by Henry Lewis Gates and others, "Dialogique Theory," by Bakhtin and others, various ethnographic and linguistic models by Schiffrin and others, or indeed any discourse model I have studied and/or used. Although Berger's model is flawed in many ways, and although it is presented in a glib fashion, it is nevertheless a powerful and rigorous model. Its power comes from its detail (45 techniques of devices) and its rigor comes from how this detail is spelled out (15 "Language" devices, 14 "Logic" devices, 13 "Identity" devices, and 3 "Action" devices.

I am deeply grateful to professor Nilsen for his kind words, which suggest that my model is of some consequence in the scholarly study of linguistics and humor.

I believe that my eliciting these 45 techniques of humor is my most important contribution to the study of humor in all its forms, such as jokes, cartoons, comic strips, situation comedies, literary comedies, and radio comedy. My argument, as Professor Nilsen pointed out in his review, is that there are 45 techniques that are used in *all* humor—no more (that I've been able to find) or no less, though my use of the technique "burlesque" has been criticized as being too broad and encompassing other techniques. We can find these techniques in ancient Greek and Roman comedies, in Shakespeare's comedies, and contemporary comedies, in many different media.

Nilsen suggests that my choice of sophisticated texts is important. As he explains (1992:97):

> The advantage of Berger's model is that it is based on sophisticated texts, and results from a close reading by a person who has a sensitive ear and an outstanding sense of humor. The texts, which are treated in detail in the book include not only Plautus' *Miles Gloriosus*, Shakespeare's *Twelfth Night*, Sheridan's *The School for Scandal*, and Ionesco's *The Bald Soprano*, to which individual chapters are devoted, but also Shakespeare's *Much Ado About Nothing*, and *Henry IV Parts I and II*, *The Merry Wives of Windsor*, Jonson's *Volpone*, Wilde's *The Importance of Being Ernest*, Beckett's *Krapp's Last Tape*, Stoppard's *Travesties*, and Griffith's *Comedians*, from which extensive supporting details are taken.

He adds a comment on my suggestion that my content analysis of a variety of different kinds of texts shows that there are only forty-five techniques, but they can be used in endless combinations. My argument is that humor, whenever it was created and wherever it is found, is built upon using the 45 techniques I elicited, often in various complex combinations and permutations. Thus, even a seemingly simple kind of text such as a joke might employ several different techniques at the same time to generate mirthful laughter. Let me offer two examples of jokes with many different techniques operating in them at the same time. I will call the first joke "The Tan."

The Tan

A man goes to Miami for a vacation. After four days, he looks in the mirror and notices he has a tan all over his body, except for his penis. He decides to remedy the situation. So the next day he goes to a deserted area of the beach early in the morning, takes his clothes off and lies down. He sprinkles sand over himself until all that remains in the sun is his penis. Two little old ladies walk by on the boardwalk and one notices the penis. "When I was 20," she says, "I was scared to death of them. When I was 40, I couldn't get enough of them. When I was 60, I couldn't get one to come near me....and now they're growing wild on the beach."

In this joke, we have several techniques at work. We have 15, Eccentricity. The man feels he must have every bit of his body tanned, even his penis. We also have 29, Mistakes. The old lady thinks that penises are growing wild on the beach. And we have 18, Exposure—in both the exhibitionism of the man and the suppressed sexual desire of the woman.

15	Eccentricity
29	Mistakes
18	Exposure

Let me offer the second joke, which is also one of my favorites. I will call this joke "The Minister and His Wife."

The Minister and His Wife

A minister returns unexpectedly early to his apartment and finds the strong smell of cigar smoke and his wife lying naked in bed. He looks out the window and sees a priest smoking a big cigar walking out of the door of his apartment house. In a jealous rage, he picks up the refrigerator and throws it on the priest, killing him instantly. Then, smitten by remorse he jumps out the window and kills himself. The next instant, the minister, the priest and a rabbi appear before an angel at the Pearly Gates. "What happened?" the angel asks the priest. "I was walking out of this house after visiting with a parishioner who is ill and a refrigerator fell on me," said the priest." "And you?" asks the angel to the minister. "I threw the refrigerator on the priest and then felt so bad I killed myself." "And you?" asks the angel to the rabbi. "You've got me," says the rabbi. "I was minding my own business...smoking a cigar in a refrigerator...."

Here we start with 11, Coincidence. The minister returns early and finds a strong smell of cigar smoke in his apartment. Then we have 29, Mistakes. He looks out the window and assumes the priest he sees, who is smoking a cigar, is the source of the cigar smoke. Finally, we have 19, Facetiousness—in which the rabbi explains that he was minding his own business, smoking peacefully in a refrigerator.

11	Coincidence
29	Mistakes
19	Facetiousness

I've used these jokes and many other jokes and other humorous texts this book because I believe that a book on humor should offer many examples of humor to explicate various points that are being made. Humor is a "serious" business, and a very complex matter, so it is imperative to offer examples of humor, when possible and relevant to the matter being discussed. Because I discuss humorous texts from several different media, in addition to jokes, I offer dialogue from situation comedies and other forms of humorous texts to enrich the discussions.

We can see from these two examples that jokes often contain several different techniques which interact with one another and, when successful, generate mirthful laughter. My argument, what Nilsen refers to as "strong claims," is that these 45 techniques are found in ancient as well as modern humorous texts and texts in different countries, so the 45 techniques are both historically timeless and universal. We know, however, that different countries laugh at different things. What happens, I suggest, is that countries select from the list of 45 techniques the ones that are most congruent with their national character and historical experience.

I use the Yiddish term "goyim" about non-Jews reluctantly because it can have negative connotations. It comes from the Hebrew term "goy" for a nation. I try to avoid it as much as possible but in some places, especially in humorous texts, it is necessary to use it.

Let me now offer a brief description of the contents of this book. The first chapter in this book is a description of my experiences writing my dissertation, *Li'l Abner.* The second article "Anatomy of the Joke," which appeared in the *Journal of Communication* in 1976, is the first article I published on humor that uses my 45 techniques. The third chapter, "How Jokes Work," deals with how scholars from different disciplines analyze a joke. The fourth chapter, "Professor Ferdinand de Saussure Goes to a Bar," on the pilot episode of the brilliant situation comedy *Cheers,* draws upon semiotic theory to show the numerous contrasts that exist in the episode among the characters.

My focus in this chapter is on how people find meaning in texts and draws upon Saussure's classic work, *Course in General Linguistics.* In this book, he explained that signs (which we can define as anything that can be used to stand for something else) are composed of *signifiers* (sounds, objects) and *signifieds* (concepts) whose relationship is arbitrary and based on convention. He also explained that the meaning of concepts is based on differences. As he wrote (1966:117) that "Concepts are purely differential and defined not by their positive content but negatively by their relations with the other terms of the system. Their most precise characteristic is in being what the others are not."

There is a line in *Cheers* in which Diane Chambers tells Sam Malone that her fiancé Sumner Sloane is "everything you're not." Since I am a semiotician, that line, of course, caught my attention. So it is the network of relationships that exist in this text, and their relation to cultural codes, that was the focus of my investigation of this text. I examined and interpreted the meaning of the most important elements in the show: the title, the location in Boston, Diane's "blondeness," the names of the characters (this part is admittedly highly speculative), the cultural codes and code violations that generate much of the humor in the episode, and the numerous oppositions found in the text. *Cheers* was one of the most successful situation comedies in the eighties and one of its characters, Frazier, was to become the lead figure in another successful situation comedy, "Frazier" which will also be analyzed later in this book. Both of these shows are available on the internet.

The next chapter in this book, "Laugh and the World Laughs With You," puts my claim that the techniques of humor are universal to a test, with some jokes from different countries. The jokes are from Iran, Argentina, Israel, America, Japan, and England and deal with many different subjects. We can't classify jokes and other humorous texts according to subjects because humor deals with an infinite number of subjects, even though a good deal of it involves sexuality. Classifying jokes according to subjects leads to a huge list of topics that does not reveal anything of significance. What I was able to show was that regardless of where the jokes came from and the subjects they deal with, they all used one or more of the 45 techniques, which explains why the expression "Laugh and the world laughs with you" has significance.

I move from a discussion of the importance of these techniques in verbal humor in chapter 6, "Arthur as a Writer, Artist and Secret Agent," which is an examination of the role of these techniques in visual humor. If the techniques are universal, as I argue, and the necessary components of all humor, they must inform visual as well as verbal humor, and in this chapter, I suggest that this is the case. I do not use the numbers of the techniques the way I did in analyzing the jokes I dealt with, but I do point out how techniques such as exaggeration, eccentricity, and caricature are found in much visual humor. I also deal with visual puns in the form of some "CON" (as in convict) cartoons I've done, such as concave, content, and condom.

There are two kinds of humorous comic strips: serial ones that exist over long periods, such as *Li'l Abner,* whose adventures sometimes lasted for weeks at a time, and what we might call "daily gag" ones that have continuing characters but end every day with a gag, such as *Peanuts* and *Dilbert.* It is possible to see these daily gag comics as similar to jokes, with the panels leading up to the final panel as functioning as the set-up parts of a joke, and the final panel as being equivalent to a punch line.

Let me offer an example from a *Dilbert* strip but present it as a joke. This strip appeared the day after one in which an extraterrestrial ate an employee in Dilbert's company.

The Merger

A worker says to his boss, "I recommend we cancel our planned merger. They [the extraterrestials] plan to open a chain of fast-food restaurants using our employees as a source of protein." His boss replies, "If we always waited for the perfect situation, we'd never get anything done."

Much of the humor in the strip comes from our following the exploits of Dilbert and the other characters over the years and the stupidity of his boss, with the pointy hair rising from his head like two horns. The episode is also a satirical comment on commonly held notions that the best is the enemy of the good and suggests that trying to achieve perfection is always foolhardy.

The focus of these chapters is on the nature of humor itself and on the way my 45 techniques inform humor of all kinds. In the remainder of the book, we move into an exploration of humor's relation to the psyche and topics such as Chapter 7, "Humor and Health." and Chapter 8, "Mediated Mirth," the exploits of a radio psychologist in *Frasier.*

My research on the relationship between humor and creativity suggests that creative people often have a well-developed sense of humor, which suggests that humor can liberate people from conventional ways of thinking. The chapter on how humor heals offers a "bio-psycho-social" perspective on the effects of humor. It starts with a discussion of the physiological and mental benefits of mirthful humor and suggests it has an intrinsically therapeutic effect on people. What is original in my argument is that it is not the subject of the humor or the kind of humor (such as jokes, cartoons, comic strips) that provides the physiological, psychological and social benefits but the techniques of humor.

We must recognize the role of chance or accident in humor. Jack Benny developed his persona as a cheapskate by chance. In my classification system, this would involve the technique of eccentricity, which I locate as a kind of humor involving identity. Benny's writers put in a cheapskate joke in a program and got such positive feedback that added more of these jokes and that led to Benny adopting the persona of a miser. This persona was then mined in various ways for its comic potentials for many decades.

In keeping with my focus on the psychological aspects of humor, in chapter eight, I discuss *Frasier,* one of the more successful situation comedies of recent years. The lead character, Frasier Crane, is a radio psychologist, who deals with calls from all kinds of comically strange and distressed people, with colleagues at his radio station who are also victims of various compulsions and other kinds of neurotic behavior, and with his effete brother Niles and their blue-collar lifestyle father Martin, a retired policeman. And with Eddie, his father's dog, who always stares at Frazier. In the radio station, Frasier works with Roz Doyle, a very beautiful woman who is man-crazy and sex-starved, and whose romantic entanglements always fail. The same applies to Frasier, who is always looking for the "right" woman and never succeeds in finding her, or if he does find her after a short while manages to alienate her one way or another.

What distinguishes this situation comedy from others is that all of the characters have a depth to them and are real, despite their eccentricities and psychological tics. So, even though we laugh at them, we often empathize with them and feel connected to them and recognize ourselves in their trials and trepidations. At the end of its run, *Frasier* became stale and lost its unique quality. When Frasier's brother Niles, who spent years being "lovesick" over Daphne Moon, his father's physical therapist, finally married her, the show became more of a domestic comedy and lost its "groove."

The pilot episode of *Frasier,* "The Good Son," was brilliant. It served to introduce the major characters and highlight their eccentricities and strange relationships. The creators of the show wanted to use the character Frasier but wanted to distance the new show from *Cheers,* which is where Frasier first made his appearance, so they moved the locale of the show across the country to Seattle and made Frasier a pompous but still humane psychiatrist and created a collection of characters to interact with him in the show, such as his even more effete brother Niles, also a psychiatrist, and his wife Maris, who we never see but always hear about. Basic to the show is a clash of different lifestyles and personality types, which the writers of the show were able to play upon for many years.

I turn next, in chapter nine, to Jewish humor which I suggest evolved as a valuable tool for Jews who were striving to survive and maintain a semblance of sanity under terrible conditions in the shtetls in Eastern Europe to which they were confined. After these chapters that focus on the psychological aspects of humor, we move into a section where the focus is more directly upon the social and political dimensions of humor. All humor has a social relevance but in some humorous texts, that aspect is not immediately evident and is of secondary importance. In this chapter "Notes on Jewish Humor," which deals with Jewish jokes, I consider the role Jewish humor has played for the Jewish people, who, except for the state of Israel, have always been marginalized and politically weak. In the United States, in the Thirties and Forties, an overwhelming proportion of the comedians were Jewish—perhaps as many as seventy or eighty percent of them. I offer some examples of Jewish humor, much of which I received over the Internet, where Jewish humor is very popular. These examples use punning and playing with language and parody to great effect and achieve their humor by ridiculing certain aspects of Jewish life.

The Jewish Haiku parodies use the Haiku form to make fun of Jewish cultural attributes and behavior. Thus, the verse:

Jewish Haiku
Beyond Valium,
the peace of knowing one's child
is an internist.

reflects the stress in Jewish culture on education and careers in the professions, especially medicine. We can contrast this with a Gentile joke:

Two Gentile Mothers

Two Gentile mothers meet on the street and start talking about their children. Gentile mother 1 (said with pride) "My son is a construction worker." Gentile mother 2 (said with more pride) "My son drives a truck."

But this self-ridicule of the Jews in Jewish humor is not to be understood as a kind of masochism but the opposite—a sense of ease that enables Jews to make fun of themselves and ridicule Gentiles as well, in the "Gentile Jokes" that I offer, which, as the example above shows, are the polar opposites to Jewish ones and reflect different cultures and values. I suggest that Jews use Gentiles as "others" who enable Jewish people to differentiate themselves from non-Jews and to help consolidate Jewish identity. While many of the professional comedians in the United States now are African Americans and Latinos, the Jewish joke still lives on the Internet (where there are almost 800,000 sites listed for "Jewish jokes") and at countless Bar Mitzvahs, Bat Mitzvahs, weddings, and other Jewish life-cycle events.

If the chapter on Jewish jokes dealt with an important kind of "ethnic" humor, the next chapter, Chapter ten, "Deconstructing a Russian Joke," which analyzes a radio Erevan joke. It is an example of the kind of political humor which flourished under the Stalinist Russian regime. Radio Erevan is a radio station in what is now Soviet Armenia and the Radio Erevan jokes are all thinly veiled attacks on Russian political and hegemonic domination of various countries. Let me offer a typical Radio Erevan joke:

Socialism in the Sahara

Someone calls Radio Erevan and asks "Would it be possible to bring Socialism to the Sahara?" "Yes," replied Radio Erevan, "But after the first Five Year Plan, we would have to important sand."

This joke, then, ridicules Russian politics and economic planning, suggesting that if Russia put one of its famous five-year plans into operation in the Sahara, it would run out of sand. In other words, everything the Russians do turns out to be a disaster. At a lecture I gave at Kinko University in Japan in May 2008, I used this joke and found that the students couldn't see anything funny about it. That shows how it takes a certain background and understanding of language and culture to understand humor. The students couldn't recognize the absurdity of having to import sand to the Sahara desert. This joke originated in Eastern Europe. Americans can see the humor in it, but for some reason, the Japanese students to whom I lectured could not.

In his book *The Structure of the Artistic Text* (Michigan Slavic Contributions, 1977: 6, 17, 23) the Russian semiotician Yuri Lotman writes:

> The tendency to interpret *everything* in an artistic text as meaningful is so great that we rightfully consider nothing accidental in a work of art... Art is the most economical, compact method for storing and transmitting information. But art has other properties wholly worth of the attention of cyberneticians and perhaps, in time, design engineers. Since it can concentrate a tremendous amount of information into the "area" of a very small text...an artistic text manifests yet another feature: it transmits different information to different readers in proportion to each one's comprehension.

Lotman's formulation explains why artistic texts, including seemingly "simple" texts such as jokes, are so complex and difficult to explicate. He also explains why different people can see different things in the same texts; the more you know, the more you can see.

Chapter eleven is an examination of an extremely popular British television comedy show in 2003, "Little Britain." The show generally contains several skits, all starring the two writers of the show, who adopt a variety of different zany and bizarre comedic personas (thanks to makeup, wigs, and costuming) that make fun of British character and culture. Many of the skits deal with certain personality types found in Britain and because it is British, many of the allusions and kinds of characters used in the skits differ from those found in American situation comedies and other comedy shows. Every week the same characters appear but always in slightly different situations, so audiences become interested in what new variation the writers will have thought up. I found the show brilliant but somehow tedious.

I deal with the comedic techniques used by the writers and performers in the show, which is another example of the way my 45 humorous techniques can be found in comedic texts in other countries. This discussion of the techniques of humor in "Little Britain" shows how my interest in the 45 techniques of humor that I elicited in a content analysis of humor that I conducted forty or so years ago informs this book and most of my work on humor. Some critics suggest that my list of 45 techniques is flawed and that there are fewer techniques. Indeed, one prominent theorist has argued that all humor is based on aggression, which would involve a number of my techniques that have an aggressive nature, such as insult, ridicule, sarcasm, and satire. Whether there is only one explanation of humor—that involves *why* we laugh, or whether my 45 techniques that explain *what makes us laugh* are valid, the subject of humor remains an enigma. In my career as a humor scholar, I would conclude by saying "further research into the role of the techniques in humor, based on sampling and analyzing as many great jokes and other examples of humor as can be found, is called for."

Chapter twelve, the last chapter, "I Laughed and Lasted," deals with my relationships with humor scholars and other academics over the years and is autobiographical. I deleted some material that was in the original article because it was redundant and didn't reflect well on my activities and writings as a humor scholar.

Acknowledgments

I would like to thank all of the publishers and presses listed below for permitting me to reprint my articles in this book. "Anatomy of the Joke," *Journal of Communication*. Summer, 1976. Oxford University. "How Jokes Work: Seven Humor Theorists in Search of a Joke: Multidisciplinary Perspectives on a Humorous Text" appeared in Arie Sover, Ed. *The Languages of Humor: Verbal, Visual, and Physical Humor*. Bloomsbury, 2018. "Mediated Mirth or *Frasier,* The Good Son," is an updated and enhanced version of my chapter on *Frasier,* "Frasier: a 20th Century Fool" that was published in my book *The Agent in the Agency,* Hampton Press, 2003. "Laugh and the World Laughs With You" was written for the *Global Media Journal: Mediterranean Edition*, an Internet journal. 2007. "Number 1, 1993. "How Humor Heals" appeared in *Europe's Journal of Psychology,* 2005. "Little Britain: An American Perspective" was in Sharon Lockyear, Ed. *Reading Little Britain.* 2010. Used by permission of Bloomsbury Press. The other chapters were are major revisions of previously published articles or new material written for this book.

Li'l Abner is a satirical American comic strip that appeared in many newspapers in the United States, Canada and Europe, featuring a fictional clan of hillbillies in the impoverished mountain village of Dogpatch, USA. Written and drawn by Al Capp (1909–1979), the strip ran for 43 years, from August 13, 1934, through November 13, 1977. The Sunday page debuted six months after the daily, on February 24, 1935. It was originally distributed by United Feature Syndicate, and later by the Chicago Tribune New York News Syndicate. Comic strips typically dealt with northern urban experiences before Capp introduced *Li'l Abner*, the first strip based in the South. The comic strip had 60 million readers in over 900 American newspapers and 100 foreign papers in 28 countries. Author M. Thomas Inge says Capp "had a profound influence on the way the world viewed the American South."

Wikipedia

Just How Bitter, Petty, and Tragic Was Comic-Strip Genius Al Capp?
Steven Heller, February 28, 2013

In the 43-year run of his satiric comic strip "*Li'l Abner,*" Al Capp not only launched iconic American characters (Abner, Daisy Mae, Mammy Yokum, Pappy Yokum, the Shmoos) and places (Dogpatch, Lower Slobbovia) but introduced lingo like "hogwash," "natcherly," and "double-whammy" into the lexicon. His legacy, though, is more complicated than that. A controversial TV and radio personality whose life took a tragic spiral downward, Capp is the subject of a spicy new biography, *Al Capp: A Life to the Contrary* (Bloomsbury, USA). Its authors, veteran biographer Michael Schumacher and underground comics pioneer Denis Kitchen, set out to highlight his talents as an artist—but found themselves inevitably also chronicling the man's dark side.

https://www.theatlantic.com/entertainment/archive/2013/02/just-how-bitter-petty-and-tragic-was-comic-strip.

Chapter 1

Writing Li'l Abner

Li'l Abner was my Ph.D. dissertation and marks the beginning of my scholarly interest in humor studies. In graduate school, I had written a paper on *Li'l Abner* for a course on American politics taught by my advisor, Mulford Q. Sibley, and when I went to see him about finding a subject for my dissertation, he suggested I add new material to the paper. I agreed and then proceeded to figure out how to write about a comic strip that had been popular for many years and was read by millions of people every day. I should add that I was in an interdisciplinary American Studies program at the University of Minnesota and had to satisfy both the social scientists and humanities professors on my thesis committee.

I wrote my dissertation in 1964 and at the time, I believe there were no dissertations on a comic strip so *Li'l Abner* was the first long-form serious academic study of a comic strip. The professor of English on my committee was not thrilled by my choice of a subject, but the social scientist professors thought it a good idea, and since Sibley, an esteemed scholar, suggested the topic, my dissertation subject was accepted.

It turned out that I had met Al Capp around 1954, when I was in Boston, staying over the Christmas holidays with my brother Jason and his wife. Capp's daughter was a student of my brother's at the Museum of Fine Arts School. My brother told me that a student of his was having a party one night in Cambridge and asked me if I'd like to go. I went to the address in Cambridge my brother gave me, knocked on the door, and Al Capp opened it. I spent a bit of time talking with him at the party. He was, at the time, associated with what you might call the liberal intelligentsia in Cambridge. Later he was to become a political reactionary with a taste for beautiful young coeds that eventually destroyed his career as a television commentator. I could never have imagined that I would be writing about *Li'l Abner* some ten years later.

In M. Thomas Inge's *Comics as Culture*, we find a definition of the comics that explains why comics are so useful to scholars:

> The comic strip may be defined as an open-ended dramatic narrative about a recurring set of characters, told in a series of drawings, often including dialogue in balloons and a narrative text, and published serially in newspapers. The daily and Sunday comic strips are part of the

reading habits of more than one hundred million people of all educational and social levels. During the first part of this century, surveys have indicated that sixty percent of newspaper readers consider the comics page the priority feature in their reading. Along with jazz, the comic strip as we know it perhaps represents America's major indigenous contribution to world culture...The comics serve as revealing reflectors of popular attitudes, tastes, and mores.

I would add that the comic strip is an art form with the following characteristics: It has dialogue that is generally in balloons (but not always); it has continuing characters; it has a narrative structure (either daily strips or in long-form episodes); it simulates sound effects via terms like ZAP, BOOM and it is made up of panels which contain visual images and textual material My drawing illustrates a number of these attributes of comic strips.

Figure 1.1. Communication Techniques in Comics

1. speech in regular balloons
2. thoughts in scalloped balloons
3. sound effects in zigzagged balloons
4. facial expressions
5. lines to indicate movement
6. panel for continuity
7. setting
8. art styles—light and dark, composition, and so on
9. language—meanings of words and punctuation
10. clothes, objects, and other examples of material culture

Communication Techniques in Comics

My colleagues in the American Studies Ph.D. program at Minnesota thought that my writing about a comic strip was frivolous, if not ridiculous. But I persevered and wrote the dissertation, whose first sentence, in the preface to the book, reads "They laughed when I sat down at the typewriter," an allusion to the famous advertisement "They laughed when I sat down at the piano." The final irony is that my dissertation on *Li'l Abner* was published by Twayne in 1969 and their dissertations languish on library shelves in the University of Minnesota library. I must admit that researching the comic strip, which was a brilliant satire, provided many good laughs.

I had spent a year as a Fulbright scholar in Milan in 1963 and met Umberto Eco and many of his colleagues, who thought that popular culture was an important subject and worth investigating. In the Appendix to my book, I discuss the writings of Italian scholars on comics (1969:182-183):

> In the January 12, 1965 issue of *Il Mondo*, an important Italian weekly that deals with politics, culture, and society, there was an article by Cesare Manuucci entitled "Sociologia del fumetto"—"The Sociology of the Comic Strip," as we would put it.
>
> In this article, Mr. Manucci mentioned that the University of Rome has recently started archives on the comics and that in conjunction with these archives, a society has been founded for the systematic study of comics. There is already in existence in Milan a similar "Comics Club," led by Umberto Eco and a group of Milanese intellectuals, whose interests also include popular culture items such as hit songs and television programs. Eco, who is Professor of Mass Communications at the University of Torino has written a remarkable study—*Apocallitici e Integrati*—dealing with how comic strips should be analyzed, both as an art form and socially and politically interesting documents.

While in Italy, I had written a chapter on American and Italian comics for Professor Agostino Lombardi's journal, *Studi Americani*. My article deals with the value of studying popular culture and compares American and Italian comics, of the same period with similar characters. I used a modification of that article as my first chapter in my dissertation. The second chapter dealt with the nature of satire and *Li'l Abner*'s place in American satire. Maybe sub-literary satire would be more accurate. I examined, among other things, the strip's roots in southwestern American folk humor. *Li'l Abner* is based in Dogpatch, a mythical hillbilly place but in some episodes, it also takes place in big cities. Abner is a big, handsome and dumb hillbilly who is taken advantage of by everyone. Abner eventually married to Daily Mae, a beautiful woman he pursued (or was pursued by) for many years, marrying her only after his hero

Fearless Fosdick got married. Abner had made an oath to do whatever Fosdick did, and Fosdick got married.

I decided that dealing with a long-running serial comic strip, which started in 1934 and ended in 1977, provided an impossibly large amount of material to deal with in-depth. I concluded it was better to select certain iconic episodes that reflected the ethos of the strip and write about them. In addition to these episodes, and I could have dealt with many more, I concluded I should deal with the basic elements of a comic strip:

Capp's use of language, which was remarkable,
Capp's narrative structure, and
Capp's graphic style.

These three elements are basic to all comic strips.

As an example of Capp's use of language, I offer the following, "Marryin' Sam's" description of what he does for an eight dollar wedding:

Fust—Ah strips t' th' waist an' rassles th' four biggest guests!! Next—a fast demon-stray-shun o' how t' cheat your friends at cards!!—followed by four snappy jokes—guaranteed t' embarrass man or beast—an' then after ah dances a jig wif a pig, Ah yanks out tow o' mah teeth and presents 'em t' th' bride an' groom—as mementos o' th' occasion!!—then—Ah really gits goin!!—Ah offers t' remove any weddin' guest's appendix, with mah bare hands—free!! Then yo spread-eagles me, fastens mah arms an' laigs t' four wild jackasses—an'—bam!! yo' fires a gun!!—While they tears me t' pieces—Ah puffawms th' wedding ceremony.

Capp's graphic style can be described as having a great deal of dialogue in the panels and an endless parade of eccentrics, zanies, fools, and swindlers. Capp is often moralistic in the strip. In one episode in the strip, about Kigmies, we find a murderer in his cell. Kigmies are masochistic animals that love to be kicked. A guard comes in and the following conversation takes place:

Prisoner: I want a KIGMY!—one dat looks like ME!!
Guard: HMPH! I thought you'd want one like th' judge that sentenced you.
Prisoner: NAH'H!! HE'S not to blame for me bein' here—th' only guy who IS t'blame is ME!! –for not going't' school, like my mudder told me!!—for hangin' around wit' that tough crowd she warned me

AGAINST!!—For t'inking my mudder didn't know th' score, an' I did.
UMPH. I richly deserve this!! (and he kicks the Kigmy.)

Over the forty-three years that the strip ran, Capp invented an incredible number of eccentric characters and had many spoofs of rich businessmen, politicians, and all kinds of other professions.

Capp often used Abner as a "hero" to solve problems characters in the strip faced. In one episode, "Zoot Suit Yokum," Capp deals with a problem Zoot Suiters faced: most Americans did not wear Zoot Suits. Abner rescues a cat from a tree, is paraded around in a car labeled "The Zoot-Suit Hero," and that leads to millions of American men abandoning their regular clothing and wearing Zoot Suits. The narrative structure (and the psychology behind the episode) is relatively simple: multi-millionaire businessmen who manufacture Zoot Suits, and are shown smoking big cigars, use Abner as a hero figure to convince American men to switch to wearing Zoot Suits. Later he is nominated for the presidency but evil conservative clothing manufacturers figure out a way to thwart Abner and eventually the Zoot Suit manufacturers go out of business. Capp uses exaggeration, irony, the revelation of ignorance, grotesques, stereotypes, and many other techniques in the episode and elsewhere in the strip.

His graphic technique, which involves stereotypes and exaggeration, also adds a satiric resonance to the strip. I would describe it as using caricature, distortion, and grotesques. Capp's line is heavy and there is a considerable amount of dialogue, with many words in the equivalent of boldface type. He was fascinated by faces and identity and has many caricatures in the strip—of social types and individuals. He also has fairly well-drawn girls in the strip to add a sexy element to it. There was what I would describe as graphic exaggeration in the strip. As I explained in my dissertation (1969:143):

> There is a pattern to Capp's graphic exaggeration. Feet and hands are usually enlarged, bodies are either extended into string bean-like shapes or short, fat, dumpling-like ones. Most of the caricaturing and grotesquery involve faces, however: noses are enlarged, twisted, made bulbous or hooked; mouths are enlarged, teeth taken out or filed into points, lips are made thick and incredibly fleshy, jaws are wildly prognathous...Despite the crudity of the drawings, and they are crude because Capp wants them that way, there is a considerable amount of expression in the faces.

On the first page of the introduction to my book, I wrote (1969:13):

> This study begins where other analyses of the comics have generally
> ended: with a serious and detailed examination of style and the way it is
> related to meaning. To my knowledge, it is the first sustained critical
> study of a single comic strip. I have chosen to write on Al Capp's *Li'l*
> *Abner"* because it is one of the few strips taken seriously by students of
> American culture and because I think the quality of Capp's imagination
> is worthy of serious examination.

When the subject of my dissertation, *"Li'l Abner,"* was announced at the
University of Minnesota graduation ceremonies by the president of the
university, in 1965, people in the audience laughed. Since then, there have been
a number of books about comic strips published and many of our most popular
films are based on comic strip superheroes such as Superman, Batman, Spider-
man and other Marvel comics superheroes and superheroines. I checked on
Google to gauge popular interest in the comics and found:

> 363,000,000 results for "comic strips" and
> 1,790,000,000 results for "comic books,"
> 50,000 results on Amazon.com books for "graphic novels."

This suggests there is an enormous amount of interest in the comics and
related art forms.

I could not have known, when I wrote my dissertation, that my using the word
"meaning" would lead me to become a semiotician, which focuses on how
people find meaning in signs of all kinds, and a discourse analyst. My
dissertation, so I understand, is seen by many popular culture scholars, as an
example of how comics, and popular culture, in general, should be analyzed.
That explains why it was republished in 1994 by the University Press of
Mississippi, which offers 140 books that deal with comics one way or another.

It would take fifty years for me to discover that I was what we now call a critical
multimodal discourse analyst. There is a reason why I didn't recognize what I
was doing. When I wrote my dissertation, critical multimodal discourse
analysis had not been developed. At the time, I identified myself as a student of
popular culture and the mass media which I was and still am.

In his most important work, *Morphology of the Folktale*, Propp's approach is uncompromisingly scientific...Drawing on the scientific interest in the folktale which emerged in Russia during the mid-nineteenth century, Propp undertakes a detailed structural analysis of 100 tales from the collection of Afanas'ev. The central idea of the work is simple and has three strands: in spite of the abundance of the variety of detail, the tales share one basic plot: this plot is constructed of thirty-one "functions" (the basic units of narratives which advance the plot) which occur in identical sequential order even though not every function is present in all the tales.

Ellis Cashmore and Chris Rojek. *Dictionary of Cultural Theorists.*

The direst calamities that befall man seem to prove that human life at its depths is inherently absurd. The comic and the tragic view of life no longer exclude each other. Perhaps the most important discovery of modern criticism is the perception that comedy and tragedy are somehow akin, or that comedy can tell us many things about our situation that even tragedy cannot.

Wylie Sypher, *Comedy*

Chapter 2

Anatomy of the Joke

Dissecting humor is an interesting operation
in which the patient usually dies.

When we laugh, we respond to messages given us—information of one sort or another, or, to be more specific, relationships which are established between persons, places, and things.

These relationships generate the humor. The difference between humor and other kinds of information is that humor establishes *incongruous* relationships (meaning) and presents them to us with a *suddenness* (timing) that leads us to laugh. Incongruity is defined here as "not harmonious, not conforming, inconsistent within itself and lacking propriety."

If we take the term incongruity to involve the general matter of *shifts*, we can explain or unify a number of ways of looking at humor, or "definitions" of humor. Table 2.1 subsumes various approaches to humor under the general heading of incongruities by making use of bipolar oppositions to characterize their approaches.

Table 2.1. Theories of humor

Theorist	Bipolar Opposition
Berger	Code violations, Acceptable/Not acceptable
Hobbes	Superior/Inferior
Bateson	Paradoxesj: Lies/Truth self-contradiction
Fry	Frames: Real/Unreal
Freud	Conscious/Unconscious
Bergson	Mechanical/Flexible

Table 2.1 might be expanded to cover irony (in which there is an incongruity between what is said and what is meant) and the figure/ground relationship. We might even describe "timing as a kind of break which enhances enjoyment," so that every aspect of a joke has (from this point of view) an incongruous, shifting aspect to it.

If we look at a joke structurally to see how the violation of codes is important and how this violation is based upon some kind of incongruity in relationships which people "see" as humorous, we find the following:

> *Elements:* acts, actions, bits of a story, or what structuralists might call a "jokeme."
> *Relationships:* incongruity established as the "punch line" via one or more of various techniques. Suddenness also a factor.
> *Humor:* consequences of the establishment of incongruous or special relationships amongst elements in an episode.

When the elements or "jokemes" (the smallest act in a humorous story or tale or skit) are incongruously resolved, we find humor. Tragedy, on the other hand, is based on a logical resolution of oppositions or elements, to have power or meaning. If the resolution is circumstantial or random, the tension generated collapses and we may have pathos or melodrama.

The codes must be quite explicit. In some cultures, mothers-in-law or old people or certain animals are not considered suitable for humorous treatment, so that American jokes about subjects sacred in other lands fall flat. Because humor is intimately connected to culture-codes, it is useful in providing insights into a society's values. Under the guise of not being taken seriously, the fool tells the truth in *Lear* and many other dramas.

Table 0.1 presents 45 different techniques to generate humor, grouped into four categories: language (the humor is verbal); logic (the humor is ideational); identity (the humor is existential); and action (the humor is physical).

Since a joke may involve many different techniques and categories of humor, "dissecting" a joke is a very complicated operation, one in which the patient almost always "dies." Let us take the following joke as an example:

The Bandaged Priest

A priest was walking down the street when two hippies who knew him came over to say hello. He was heavily bandaged so one hippie said: "How did you get hurt bad enough to require such a bandage?" "Oh, it was nothing," replied the priest. "I slipped in my bath. But it is fine now and no trouble." The hippies said they were sorry he was injured and walked away. A half-block down the street the first hippie turned to the second and asked: "What's a bath?" A block later the second hippie turned to the first and said, "How should I know...I ain't Catholic."

The joke involves the following "jokemes":
1. Hippies meet priest
2. Hippies ask about bandages
3. Priest explains he slipped in his bath
4. Hippies leave priest
5. First hippie askes second what a bath is
6. Second hippie says he doesn't know
7. Second hippie explains he isn't Catholic.

The humor is based on several different techniques. First, it uses *stereotypes* (identity), in this case, the popularly held notion that hippies are dirty. Second, it uses the *revelation of ignorance* (logic); the first hippie doesn't know what a bath is and neither does the second hippie. Third, it has a *double-punch line* (language) which involves leading the listener on, for after the second hippie says "I don't know," we assume mistakenly that the joke is over. Fourth, the second hippie shows his ignorance by assuming that baths are connected with Catholicism.

The hippies are comic characters because they violate many American codes, the symbol for all of which is the basic code of cleanliness. Mistakes are part of the general area of "comedy of error," and it is the incongruity between reality and what the hippies believed that generates much of the humor. In this particular case, the listener is also duped, so the joke is on hin/her also.

The more complicated a joke is, naturally, the more difficult it is to unravel. But separating a joke into its elements and probing these elements does tell us how a humorist works.

During the unfolding of humor, one is suddenly confronted by an explicit-implicit reversal when the punch line is delivered. The reversal helps distinguish humor from play, dreams, etc. Sudden reversals such as characterize the punch line moment in humor are disruptive and foreign to play, etc.... But the reversal also has the unique effect of forcing upon the humor participants an internal redefining of reality. Inescapably, the punch line combines communication and metacommunication.

William Fry. *Sweet Madness: A Study of Humor*

It is relatively easy to discuss what a joke is, what are the characteristics that make a joke, what is the point of the joke. The sort of analysis that I want to propose assumes that the messages in the first phase of telling the joke are such that while the informational content is, so to speak, on the surface, the other content types are implicit in the background. When the point of a joke is reached, suddenly this background material is brought into the attention and a paradox, or something like that is touched off. A circuit of contradictory notions is completed.

Gregory Bateson, "The Position of Humor in Human Communication."

Chapter 3

How Jokes Work:

Six Humor Theorists in Search of a Jewish Joke (A Multi-Disciplinary Perspectives on a Humorous Jewish Text)

In recent years we have recognized that all disciplines have important limitations. That explains why there is so much interest now in interdisciplinary, multi-disciplinary or trans-disciplinary approaches to topics. When we deal with the mysteries of creative texts, the limitations of single disciplinary approaches become quite apparent: do we focus on:

the work of art (the text),

the artists (the creators of the text),

the audience of the text,

the society in which the text is found or

the medium which is used to distribute the text.

I would like to suggest the advantages of a multi-disciplinary approach to the arts and culture by taking a "simple" text, a Jewish joke, and showing how scholars from different disciplines might analyze it. I put the term "simple" in quotes because jokes are, it turns out, extremely complicated kinds of texts.

Humor, of all kinds, is a topic that has fascinated some of the greatest minds throughout history, from Aristotle to Freud, and one about which there are many different explanations and theories. I define a joke as a short narrative, with a punch line, meant to create mirthful laughter.

We can diagram a joke as follows: Each segment of the joke will be given a letter from the alphabet. In this joke, sentence E is the punchline.

A →   B →   C →   D →   E (punch line)

                                               ↓

                                    F (mirthful laughter)

One interesting thing we have to consider is that while each of our scholars from different disciplines will interpret the joke in different ways, they will all laugh—if the joke is a good one and is told well. That is because funny jokes make us laugh, but why we laugh at a funny joke, what makes a joke "funny," is the subject of many theories.

The Nature of Jewish Humor

Since this chapter is about Jewish jokes, let me say something about what is distinctive about Jewish humor. In a special edition of the journal *Humor: International Journal of Humor Research*, an Israeli humor scholar, Avner Ziv, discusses what it distinctive about Jewish humor. He writes (1991:145):

> Jewish humor is the humor created by Jews, reflecting aspects of Jewish life. This broad definition includes popular verbal humor such as jokes, or anecdotes (collected by folklorists), as well as humor created by professionals. Therefore, popular Jewish jokes collected by folklorists, Shalom Aleichem's writings, and parts of Neil Simon's plays and Woody Allen's movies are all examples of Jewish humor. Since humor reflects a people's life, it changes and varies accordingly. Thus one can talk about Eastern European, Sephardic, American or Israeli Jewish humor. In spite of the great differences in the life conditions of these different communities, Jewish humor has certain characteristics that make it unique.

A page later in the article he discusses the main psychological characteristics of Jewish humor, which are, he suggests (1991:146):

> 1:
> An intellectual dimension: a desire to distort the reality, to alter it and make it laughable (and thus less frightening and threatening). Reducing the awful reality into absurdity is a cognitive process by which one tries to make life more tolerable.
> 2:
> A social dimension: trying to maintain internal cohesiveness and identity. By comparing "us" with "them" it is possible to show that even if in reality "they" are stronger, we can still win, mainly by using our wits.
> 3:
> An emotional aspect: helping one to see oneself as one is, namely far from perfect. Making fun of some unsavory aspect of one's behavior and personality might help in accepting them. It can even show that they are not so terrible: the proof—I can even laugh at them. Another emotional aspect related to self-disparagement is the sympathy one earns from

others, and being accepted is, and was for two thousand years, a serious problem for a wandering people.

Anyone interested in a more complete analysis of Jewish humor can read my book, *The Genius of the Jewish Joke*, which argues that when Jews make fun of themselves, they are not being masochistic but just the opposite and Jewish humor reflects a triumphal sensibility. Jewish humor is about Jews—often about rabbis, about Jewish culture, about Jewish personality types and other aspects of Jewish social experience. It is about the experience of a people who are always marginal in some country, except for Israel. Jews, we must realize, make up less than two percent of the population in the United States.

Now, let me analyze a Jewish joke that I heard recently and which struck my attention, in part because it has a Muslim character in it. What I will do now is "tell" a joke and then analyze it from the perspective of several disciplines. The title of my joke is:

A Priest, an Imam, and a Rabbi Get a Haircut

A barber is sitting in his shop when a priest enters. "Can I have a haircut?" the priest asks. "Of course," says the barber. The barber then gives the priest a haircut. When the barber has finished, the priest asks "How much do I owe you?" "Nothing," replies the barber. "For you are a holy man." The priest leaves. The next morning, when the barber opens his shop, he finds a bag with one hundred gold coins in it." A short while later, an Imam enters the shop. "Can I have a haircut?" he asks. "Of course," says the barber, who gives the Imam a haircut. When the barber has finished, the Imam asks "How much do I owe you?" "Nothing," replies the barber. "For you are a holy man." The Imam leaves. The next morning, when the barber opens his shop, he finds a bag with a hundred gold coins in it." A bit later, a rabbi walks in the door. "Can I have a haircut?" the rabbi asks. "Of course," says the barber, who gives the rabbi a haircut. When the haircut is finished, the rabbi asks, "How much do I owe you?" "Nothing," replies the barber, for you are a holy man." The rabbi leaves. *The next morning, when the barber opens his shop, he finds a hundred rabbis.* (Punch line in italics)

The punch line, "*The next morning, when the barber opens his shop, he finds a hundred rabbis*, is meant to elicit mirthful laughter in those who hear the joke or read it. Let's consider, now, how scholars from different disciplines would interpret this joke. These analyses will all be brief and show what scholars with different perspectives deal with when they analyze a joke or any text.

A Rhetorical Analysis

For our purposes, the rhetorician will focus on the techniques used to generate the humor in this text. I dealt with these techniques in considerable detail in my books *An Anatomy of Humor, Blind Men and Elephants,* and *The Art of Comedy Writing.* I also offer them in a numbered alphabetical organized chart which will be useful in showing the techniques used in a given joke or other kinds of humorous texts.

We often find many different techniques in a joke, though there is usually one dominant technique. The most important technique in the joke about the priest, the imam, and rabbi, I would suggest, is one I call **43: Stereotypes**. Stereotypes are notions people have about what members of certain countries, groups, races, and religions are like. They can be positive, negative or mixed. The mechanisms behind negative stereotypes often involve 25: Insults--In this case, the negative stereotype of the cheap Jew. There is also **19: Facetiousness**. The notion that a hundred rabbis would show up in a barbershop to get a free haircut is not a serious one. In this joke, we find **34: Repetition**, in which we read about the haircuts of the priest, the imam and then the rabbi. And finally, in this joke, we find **17: Exaggeration**, in which one holy man is replaced by 100 Jewish holy men.

The main techniques found in this joke are:

43: Stereotypes.	In this case, the cheap Jew
19: Facetiousness.	A hundred rabbis is a ridiculous notion.
34: Repetition.	We find out about haircuts of the priest, the imam and finally the rabbi.
17: Exaggeration	Having 100 rabbis show up at a barbershop.

What we find, then, is that there are at least three different techniques of humor operating in this joke to generate mirthful laughter. One might find other techniques at work in this joke, as well.

A Semiotic Analysis

One of the important techniques semioticians use when they deal with narrative texts is to consider their paradigmatic structure--the set of oppositions found in them (some would say read into them) that give them meaning. The other approach, which focuses on the syntagmatic or linear structure in texts, is based on Vladimir Propp's *Morphology of the Folktale* and makes use of his stress on the "functions" of characters to analyze any narrative text.

Ferdinand de Saussure, one of the founding fathers of semiotics, argued that concepts have meaning due to their relationships, with other concepts; nothing has meaning in itself. As he wrote in his book *Course in General Linguistics* (1915/1966: 117), "concepts are purely differential and defined not by their positive content but negatively by their relations with the other terms of the system." And the most important relationship between concepts is that of opposition. Thus, a paradigmatic or binary analysis of this joke would yield the following set of oppositions:

Non-Jewish	Jewish
Priest, Imam	Rabbi
Generous	Cheap
Leaves 100 gold coins	Sends 100 Rabbis

Listeners to the joke don't necessarily bring this set of oppositions to mind, but they must recognize them if the joke is to make any sense and the punch line is to be effective. The great French anthropologist Claude Lévi-Strauss was a champion of this mode of analyzing texts and used it with the Oedipus myth.

A Communication Theorist

In this analysis, I deal with Roman Jakobson's model, which involves a sender, a receiver, a contact (or medium), a code and a message—in this case, a joke.

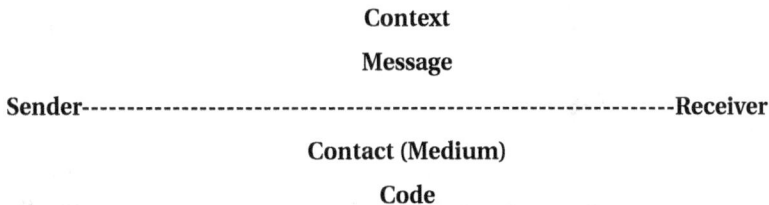

Context

Message

Sender---**Receiver**

Contact (Medium)

Code

The Jakobson Model of Communication

According to some communications theorists, a message has information to the extent that it has some kind of a surprise. This means that all jokes since they have punch lines (that are surprises) contain information. In this joke, the information conveyed by the punch line is that the rabbi and Jews are cheap.

I also deal with the matter of avoiding aberrant decoding, a situation in which a person does not interpret a message the way the sender wants the message to be interpreted. For a joke to work, the receiver or addressee must understand the message and have the same assumptions the sender has. Thus, in the punch line, when we learn about 100 Rabbis arriving at the barbershop, we must hold stereotypes of what Jews are like and understand the event and interpret it correctly.

A Psychological and Psychoanalytic Theorist

From the psychological and psychoanalytic perspective, it is the way the rabbi who gets a haircut feels about money that is of paramount importance. The heroes (or victims) of this little story are the priest, the imam, and the rabbi and the hundred rabbis he sends to get free haircuts at a barbershop. The fact that this joke, told by Jews, pokes fun of Jews can be seen as an example of the ways Jews can make fun of themselves and reflects, I would argue, a triumph of the ego over the superego and the absurdist approach to life that served Jewish people well over the years.

This laughter this joke generates can be seen as "liberating" in that it leads to the release of endorphins and thus generates a feeling of wellbeing in people. We now know that humor of all kinds has intrinsic therapeutic value, which may explain why so many people feel the need to experience humor daily. Freud's book on humor, in addition to offering a psychoanalytic approach to humor, has many wonderful Jewish jokes in it.

A Sociological Analyst

We might ask "What are the functions of this joke for the teller and the listener?" Many sociologists use functional analysis to make sense of human behavior. Functionalists are concerned about whether some behavior helps maintain an institution in which it is found (is functional), causes problems for the institution in which it is found (is dysfunctional) or plays no role in the institution (nonfunctional). Functions also can be recognized (manifest functions) or not recognized (latent functions). Let me suggest some functions related to humor.

Telling the joke helps build a sense of togetherness, helps integrate the joke teller and the listeners into a group (those listening to the joke). The manifest or overt function of telling the joke is to amuse others, to be looked upon favorably as someone who has a sense of humor, who is amusing and entertaining. The latent function may be to deal with sexual anxieties and repression? And also to show human fallibility at many different levels and to help release us from the burdens of a very strict morality. The Jews who tell this joke and laugh are showing they are liberated from the constraints of a dominating superego. Laughter is a means of liberation.

A Philosopher of Humor

Philosophers have generally concerned themselves with the nature of humor in general, its ontological status, and that kind of thing. Aristotle argued that we laugh at people we see as ridiculous, as inferior to ourselves. He is one of the fathers of the "superiority" theory of humor. From this perspective, the humor in the joke comes from our being able to feel superior to the minister and his wife, the priest and the rabbi.

Henri Bergson argued that humor involves "the mechanical encrusted on the living" and suggested that this manifests itself in many ways, one of which was comic types. By this, he meant people who are fixated, rigid, inflexible...such as misers, misanthropes, etc. Wherever you have a type, he wrote, you have humor. The rabbi in this joke represents a comic type—a frugal, or some may say cheap or miserly person. Instead of giving the barber one hundred coins, he sends him one hundred rabbis.

A Political Scientist

A political scientist, Aaron Wildavsky, has suggested, in several essays and books, that there are four political cultures found in democratic societies (he revised things and added a fifth one, but it is small and not significant for our purposes). These cultures are formed due to the number of the rules and prescriptions groups placed on members of groups (few or many) and the strength or weakness of the boundaries that exist among groups (weak or strong). The chart below shows these relationships.

Political Culture	Group Boundaries	Number and Kinds of Rules
Hierarchical Elitist	Strong	Numerous
Egalitarian	Strong	Few
Individualist	Weak	Few
Fatalist	Weak	Many

We end up with four political cultures: egalitarians, (hierarchical) elitists, (competitive) individualists and fatalists. Mary Douglas who thought up this kind of analysis called the groups "lifestyles." People sometimes change political cultures and are not locked into a given group for life, though fatalists generally find it difficult to escape from that position.

I argue, pushing things to extremes perhaps, that a given joke, based on the values it supports or attacks, should appeal primarily to one of these political cultures (or people moving toward a given political culture) since it reinforces their beliefs. Conversely, it should not appeal to the other groups since it attacks their values and generates cognitive dissonance.

In this context, the joke would be seen as essentially an egalitarian one, since it presents miserliness or cheapness in a relatively benign or comedic manner. And there are few rules to hamper the egalitarian's behavior. The joke, we might say, "normalizes" cheapness and, by doing so, appeals to egalitarian values, which stress the things that people have in common rather than those that divide them, and the equality of needs we all have. An elitist joke would have made the rabbi an object of strong ridicule and suggested that cheapness is a grave matter. A fatalist joke would have suggested that the rabbi's economic status was a matter of bad luck And a competitive individualist joke might involve something like seeing who could be cheaper: a priest, an imam or a rabbi.

We must also remember that humor can be used to control people (especially in small groups) or to resist control. The joke might be seen as a means of resisting the power of the elites and the moral strictures dominant in a given society.

Conclusions

Jewish humor is tied to distinctive aspects of Jewish culture and it is not the subject matter that Jewish jokes deal with that is important but the Jewish cultural sensibility. In the early days, in Europe, Jews engaged in pilpul in their yeshivas and developed a capacity to see things in many different ways and a facility with language that could easily be turned into a humorous perspective on things. That might explain why something like eighty percent of the comedians in the United States, many years ago, were Jewish. And why there are so many Jewish lawyers.

This brings us to the end of our exercise. I have tried to suggest how each perspective, discipline, theory, methodology (or whatever) might make sense of the joke about the priest, the imam, and the rabbi getting a haircut. Each perspective examines the joke in different ways, and while a joke may not be completely illuminated by a given perspective, it does offer important insights which, when put together with other ones, does a good job of explaining and interpreting the joke in a relatively complete and interesting manner.

Note: If you are interested in pursuing this approach, my book *Blind Men and Elephants* offers extended analyses of humor from many different disciplinary perspectives. My book *The Art of Comedy Writing* deals with theatrical comedies and the techniques used by the writers of these works, and my book *An Anatomy of Humor* discusses the techniques, offers examples of humor for each technique, and analyzes some humorous texts.

References

Berger, Arthur Asa. (1993) *An Anatomy of Humor.* New Brunswick, NJ: Transaction.

Berger, Arthur Asa. (1995) *Blind Men and Elephants: Perspectives on Humor.* New Brunswick, NJ: Transaction.

Berger, Arthur Asa. (1997) *The Art of Comedy Writing.* New Brunswick, NJ: T transaction

Berger, A.A. and Wildavsky, A. "Who Laughs at What?" *Society* 31, 82-86. 1994.

Bergson, Henri. (1911) *Laughter: An Introduction.* London: MacMillan.

Douglas, Mary. (1975) "Jokes" *in Implicit Meanings: Essays in Anthropology.* Routledge & Kegan Paul.

Propp, Vladimir. (1968) (2nd edition) *Morphology of the Folktale.* Austin, TX: University of Texas Press.

Wildavsky, A. (1982). "Conditions for a pluralist democrazy, or cultural pluralism means more than one political culture in a country. Unpublished manuscript, University of California-Berkeley, Department of Political Science.

Ziv, Avner (1991:145) *Humor International Journal of Humor Research.*

Language is a system of signs that express ideas and is therefore comparable to a system of writing, the alphabet of deaf-mutes, symbolic rites, polite formulas, military signals, etc. But it is the most important of all these systems. *A science that studies the life of signs within society* is conceivable; it would be a part of social psychology and consequently of general psychology; I shall call it *semiology* (from Greek *sēmeîon* "sign"). Semiology would show what constitutes signs, what laws govern them. Since the science does not yet exist, no one can say what it would be; but it has a right to existence, a place staked out in advance.

Ferdinand de Saussure, *Course in General Linguistics*

The basic unit of semiotics is the *sign* defined conceptually as something that stands for something else, and, more technically, as a spoken or written word, a drawn figure, or a material object unified in the mind with a particular cultural concept. The sign is this unity of word-object, known as a *signifier* with a corresponding, culturally prescribed content or meaning, known as a *signified*. Thus our minds attach the word "dog," or the drawn figure of a "dog," as a signifier to the idea of a "dog," that is, a domesticated canine species possessing certain behavioral characteristics. If we came from a culture that did not possess dogs in daily life, however unlikely, we would not know what the signifier "dog" means. . . .

Mark Gottdiener, The *Theming of America: Dreams, Visions, and Commercial Spaces.*

Chapter 4

Professor Ferdinand de Saussure

Goes to a Bar

Imagine what would happen if Professor Ferdinand de Saussure, one of the founding fathers of semiotics, the science of signs (he called his theory semiology) went into a bar in Boston. The bar he went into was called *Cheers*. And he observed the events taking place in that bar for the first or pilot episode of the show. What sense would he make of the events that transpired in that bar?

A sign, semioticians tell us, is anything that can stand for something else. Words and objects are signs. So are facial expressions, gestures, body language, hairstyles and hair colors, brands of things we wear or purchase such as smartphones or running shoes. What semiotics does is try to figure out how signs communicate their meaning and how people make sense of signs. When we watch a television show, we listen to what the characters say, we notice the tone of their voices (sarcastic? abrasive?) we watch how they walk, we scrutinize their facial expressions, we consider their body language and their gestures. We are affected by the kinds of shots in the show, by the music, by how the characters are dressed, by their bodies and many other things. What we are doing is functioning as amateur semioticians. From the moment we are born, we spend a great deal of time learning how to make sense of all the signs around us.

Technically, Saussure explained that signs have two parts:

a *signifier* (a sound, an object, a facial expression, etc.) and
a *signified* (what the sign means)

The relationship that exists between a signifier (you have a new Mercedes) and its signified (you love German engineering and are prosperous enough to own a Mercedes) is arbitrary and based on convention. You actually may not own it and be renting it, giving people false impressions of your financial status. Signs can change their meaning. For example, long hair on men fifty years ago meant "artist, musician, etc." and now long hair on men doesn't mean anything.

The basic question that semiology (or semiotics or structuralism) asks of a television program or film or advertisement—or any "text"—Is this: How do people understand what's going on? How do people derive meaning from a text? How do they know how to interpret facial expressions, body movements, clothes the characters wear, kinds of shots, the scenery, correctly? How is meaning generated and conveyed?

Jonathan Culler, a semiotician, wrote a book, *Structuralist Poetics* in which argued that (1976:4)

> first, that social and cultural phenomena aren't simply material objects or events but objects and events with meaning, and hence signs and second, that they do not have essences but are defined by a network of relations.

Meaning, Culler tells us, stems from considering phenomena as signs and from looking at the relationships among these signs.

Relationships are basic which means, among other things, that signs can lie. Short men can "lie" about their height by wearing certain shoes that make them look taller. Women with dark hair can "lie" about themselves by becoming blondes.

The most important relationship in language, for our concerns, is that of a polar or binary opposition, which is the fundamental way in which the human mind finds meaning. In essence, we search for the hidden set of oppositions that inform a text and thus generate meaning. This meaning is not necessarily recognized by people but it is there nevertheless, and can be elicited by the semiotician. If this is the case, we can make sense of the pilot episode of *Cheers* by examining the signs that inform the show and by finding the oppositions in them that give the show meaning.

Signs in the Show

The title of the show, *Cheers* suggests happiness, good spirits (in this case literally as well as figuratively), and companionship since "cheers" is a toast we often make when we are drinking with others. So we have expectations from the name of the show about what it will be about.

Boston

The *Cheers* bar itself is a sign or more precisely, a collection of signs. It is not drab or shabby, like a working-class bar nor is it a fancy, trendy bar. It seems to be a neighborhood bar that caters mainly to middle-class people. The bar and the row of liquor bottles we find in it are signifiers of what the French semiotician Roland Barthes would have called "barness." The bar is in Boston, which gives it a certain identity, because of the way Boston is perceived by many Americans. Boston's identity is due, in part, to its being on the East coast and closely identified with English culture, the revolutionary period, and Harvard University. Bostonians are thought to be somewhat effete and a bit snobbish—though this is reserved for upper class, (White Anglo Saxon Protestant) types and certainly not for the Irish working-class people you find there. The fact that this series takes place in Boston also prepares us for the eccentrics, weirdos, and con artists one finds in the show.

Names

Diane's name has a mythological root (in mythology her name is Artemis, a virgin huntress associated with the moon.) So Diane is well named, since her role in the show is that of an object of sexual desire, a child-like (in many senses) woman who becomes involved in a battle of the sexes with the hero, Sam. Sam's name does not tell us much, though we might be able to make something of the fact that we can find the world "alone" in Malone and it is his status as a male with no ties to a woman that facilitates his battle with Diane.

Carla Tortelli is another matter; in her name, we find "tort," which is a description of her argumentative personality. She is an injured party (her husband left her with four children) and she is bitter about her situation. Even Sumner Sloane's name is interesting, for he is, in effect, "on loan" to Diane from his ex-wife Barbara. Barbara takes him back when Sumner goes to get a ring from her. Norm and well-named; he is an everyman figure, a representation of the typical American bar patron, drinking beer, the beverage of the common man. Coach is a different matter; his name is used ironically. He is not a guide and teacher but, instead, a somewhat daffy character who cannot remember his name and is always confused.

I cannot argue that the names of the characters were made deliberately by the writers with what I've suggested and are thus of semiological/semiotic significance. But it is interesting (and maybe more than purely coincidental) that the characters have the names they do. The writers of the series are educated and bring in many names from "elite culture," such as Soren Kierkegaard and Friedrich Nietzsche (to show that Diane is an intellectual). It wouldn't be too much of a stretch of the imagination to assume that there was some conscious thought about the names of the characters.

Blondeness

The color of Diane Chambers's hair is a very important sign since blondeness is a sign of considerable richness and meaning. America is a country where "gentlemen prefer blondes," and blonde hair coloring is the most popular color sold. But what does blondeness signify? It is, for many women, a means of escaping their age and their ethnic and racial identity. Charles Winick in his book *The New People* explains:

> For a substantial number of women, the attraction of blondeness is less an opportunity to have more fun than the communication of a withdrawal of emotion, a lack of passion. One reason for Marilyn Monroe's enormous popularity win that she was less a tempestuous temptress than a non-threatening child. The innocence conveyed by blonde hair is also suggested by the 70 percent of baby dolls whose hair is blonde.

In works of fiction, blondes also tend to be vindictive and frigid. This innocence of the blonde is appealing to men because blondes, not being experienced (in theory) would not be very judgmental about men's sexual performance. Thus, when Sumner calls Diane a "child," there is more significance to the term than we might imagine.

We know that Diane and Sumner are intellectuals from the book that Diane attempts to read and her numerous allusions to material from great literary figures. And the lack of a "proper" response (awe, respect) by Sam and his friends to Sumner is an indication of their status as non-intellectuals. They are more interested in the Boston Patriots than in Andrew Marvel and linebackers for than in literary giants.

Culture Codes

If the relationship between signifiers and signifieds in signs is arbitrary, we must have codes which provide rules for interpreting things, since these codes help tell us what signs mean. What complicates matters is that different groups and subgroups have different codes so at times there is code confusion between a creator or user of a sign and an interpreter or a receiver of a sign. Thus we have the problem of what Umberto Eco calls "aberrant decoding." Codes are connected to culture and social class to a great degree which means that people who watch *Cheers* may not always "get" everything the writers have put into the show. Or some people, at least.

Also, sometimes the characters do not understand one another which is a source of the humor in numerous cases. I believe that humor is often connected to code contusion and code violations. The difference between what one expects (knowing the code) and what one gets (due to code confusion and violation) generates laughter. We often find that the characters in *Cheers* do not understand one another and, in like manner, it is reasonable to suggest that the audience of *Cheers* does not understand everything that goes on in the episode. Still, the audience probably gets a lot of the humor--or large enough audiences do—for the series to be very successful.

I will now consider the codes of *Cheers*. First, we know we are watching a comedy and thus we are prepared to laugh, to give everything a nonserious. humorous interpretation. So we watch the program with expectations that affect the way we interpret the events in the episode and relate to the characters and their activities. Since *Cheers* is a comedy, we are not surprised to see the comic types play against one another; we are prepared for the weirdos, zanies, and eccentrics who are generally found in comedies and who often represent "types" rather than being three-dimensional characters.

In this episode of *Cheers*, much of the humor comes from misunderstandings and misinterpretations made by the various characters, though there are also some "nonresponses." These two forms of code violation come from the different social and cultural backgrounds of the characters. Diane and Sumner are highly educated, middle-class types, whereas the rest of the characters are working-class and presumably less educated. So, when Carla mentions that she helped put her husband through school, Diane assumes "school" means a university, not a television repair academy. And when Coach talks about "working six years on his novel," Diane asks, incredulously, whether he's writing a novel. She discovers, instead, that he's reading one. At the root of these misunderstandings, we find cultural and socio-economic class differences.

Diane may be intelligent, but she doesn't have much common sense. The same thing can be said about Sumner, who leaves his young fiancé Diane to retrieve a ring from his ex-wife and then ends up abandoning her.

Non-responses are also a powerful form of humor. We expect a certain response and when we don't find it, we are amused. One example of "nonresponse" is found in the scene where Sumner has just introduced himself and informed Sam that he is "professor of world literature at Boston University." Sam says nothing; he refuses to "validate" Sumner, a response that people to whom I have shown the program find hilarious. Sam's nonresponse is seen as proper because Sumner is so pompous and we are pleased when he is deflated.

I offer some codes and violations found in the pilot episode which shows how important this phenomenon is.

Table 4.1. Codes and Violations

Code	Violation
Propriety	Diane, as a waitress, sits with patrons
Egalitarianism	Sam's nonresponse to Sumner's identification of himself as a professor
Loyalty	Sumner jilts Diane
Law	Kid in episode tries to get a drink with false identification.
Self-awareness	Coach doesn't even know his name
Logic	An alcoholic owns a bar
Normalcy	Eccentric types found in *Cheers*

Codes and Violations in Pilot of Cheers

For viewers to understand this episode fully, they must recognize the violations of the codes, which means they must be able to interpret facial expressions and other signs, understand motivations, and assess the behavior of the characters. This means that viewers must bring a great deal of prior knowledge to the text; and the more they know, the more they will understand. We must see *Cheers* as a figure to be interpreted against the ground of American culture and society which from our perspective, can also be seen as a collection of codes. When we watch "Cheers," we are, from a semiotic perspective, decoding a text.

The term "text" is used in academic parlance for any creative work such as a joke, an advertisement, a film, a television show, a video, a short story, a novel, a documentary, and so on. We use the term because it is convenient and saves us from having to repeat the names of the works we are dealing with.

Bipolar Oppositions

Professor Saussure, let us recall, stressed the importance of oppositions in language and our lives; his theories also apply to creative texts of one kind or another. Semiotics is, we must recognize, one of the most important tools used by scholarly film critics, television critics and anyone else interested in analyzing texts. Saussure explained that oppositions are a basic means by which we find meaning because nothing has meaning in itself. It is the network of relationships that is crucial to the generation of meaning. Let us consider some of the relations look at some oppositions between characters in *Cheers* such as between Diane and the main characters in *Cheers* and, in the episode I am writing about, between Diane and Sam, Diane and Carla, and Sam and Sumner Sloane. Here's what Professor de Saussure would find in analyzing the pilot episode of the show.

Table 4.2. Diane Chambers and Sam Malone Oppositions

Diane Chambers	Sam Malone
Female	Male
Blonde	Dark hair
Middle-class	Working class
Vulnerable	Worldly
Beauty	Beast (magnificent pagan)
Worker	Boss
Useless	Handy

Lead Character Oppositions in Pilot Episode

A basic theme in the series involves the "battle of the sexes" between Sam and Diane, who are attracted to each other but refuse to admit it. One law of situation comedies is that in "battle of the sexes" comedies, the protagonists cannot get married lest the series become a "domestic comedy," so Sam and Diane spend their time flirting, often becoming involved in situations from which they extricate themselves with great difficulty. That is their fate. We do not know this when we see the pilot, but we can presume this will be the case from our knowledge of the genre and the logic of the situation.

Next, Professor Saussure turns to another interesting opposition: the one that exists between Diane and Carla.

Table 4.3. Diane and Carla Oppositions

Diane	Carla
Tall	Short
Blonde	Dark hair
Single (to be married)	Was married (now single)
Cool/reserved	Hot/bitchy
Middle-class	Working class
WASP	Ethnic
Innocent	Experienced
(Schoolmarm)	(Bargirl)

Diane and Carla Oppositions

We can see that these two characters are opposites in many important respects and those differences help contribute to the comedy. The same can be said for Sam Malone and Sumner Sloane.

Table 4.4. Sam and Sumner Oppositions

Sam Malone	Sumner Sloane
Tall	Short
Young	Old
Jock	Egghead
Modest	Pompous
Regular guy	Goof
Common sense	Intelligence
The world	The academy
Hires Diane	Abandons Diane

Sam and Sumner Oppositions

We can suggest that Sumner's character is defined by how different he is from Sam. In one scene, Diane says, in an important line spoken to Sam, that Sumner is "everything you're not." And this is quite true. Sumner is an egg-head, an intellectual, but like many intellectuals as they are portrayed in the popular media, he lacks common sense and morality—he abandons Diane after being "mesmerized" by his former wife, Barbara. He is a highly stereotyped figure: academics are conventionally seen as intelligent but unworldly, lacking common sense and often lacking decency. Sam has no problem in immediately sizing Sumner up as a "goof."

This polarity between the uneducated by naturally "wise" common man and the intelligent but impractical and unworldly scholar has deep roots in American culture and can be found in the early 1800s in our idealization of the various "nature's noblemen" with whom we identified. It is connected to ideas we had about ourselves and the way we contrasted ourselves with Europeans.

The following set of oppositions between American and European culture and values shows the way we think about ourselves and not the way we actually were or are.

Table 4.5. America and Europe Polar Oppositions

America	Europe
Nature	History
Individualism	Conformity
Innocence	Guilt
The Future	The Past
Hope	Memory
Forests	Cathedrals
Cowboy	Cavalier
Willpower	Class Conflict
Equality	Hierarchy
Achievement	Ascription
Classless Society	Class-Bound
Natural Raw Food	Gourmet Food
Clean Living	Sensuality
Action	Theory
Agrarianism	Industrialism
The Sacred	**The Profane**

Bipolar Oppositions and American Culture

This chart represents our commonly held notions about how Americans differ from Europeans and it helps explain many of the codes we find in *Cheers* and our mediated texts, in general.

In essence, we see ourselves as innocent, wise, egalitarian, individualistic characters living in a classless society in a state of nature, which can be contrasted with Europeans, whom we see as guilt-ridden, trained conformists living in a hierarchically organized society dominated by institutions such as the church and nobility. Sam is shown as a classic American "regular guy" figure, and Sumner is portrayed as a European-like elitist character. The fact that he is a professor of world literature suggests his lack of Americanness and that he has, somehow, been tainted by exposure to European culture.

In addition to the oppositions that exist among the characters, there is a central set of oppositions in the text that is worth considering. These oppositions involve characters but have broader implications.

Table 4.6. Main Oppositions in Pilot of Show

Youth	Adulthood
Kids who can't drink	Grown-ups who can drink
Young teaching assistant	Old(er) professor
Working-class	**Middle Class**
Workers, patrons	Sumner Sloane, Diane Chambers
The Future	**The Past**
The marriage	Ex-baseball player
Grad student	Ex-wife of Sumner
Con Artists	**Marks**
The Kid	Sam
Sumner's ex-wife	Sumner
Inside	**Outside**
The bar	The outside world
Regulars	Strangers, aliens
The Beauty	**The Beast**
Diane	Sam

Oppositions in Pilot Episode of Cheers

These oppositions are of central importance in the pilot episode—and the whole series. It is a "battle of the sexes," and a whole series of other confrontations that generate not only dramatic interest and tension but also humor, because the possibilities for misunderstanding and misinterpretation, are enormous.

Identification with Characters

There is a different kind of opposition worth mentioning here which involves the difference between the main characters, who will appear in each episode, and the various characters, such as Sumner Sloane, who will be seen in only one episode. As we watch the series, we will get to know the main characters, and the series will function as a kind of "ground" that will help us interpret what these characters do and understand them better. They will have a different "status" than the characters who appear for an episode and then disappear. The one time characters will remain more stereotyped and one-dimensional; we can understand their behavior because they will be "types," with conventional signs and codes. With each episode the main characters, even though they may be stereotyped, will become more real and multi-dimensional because they will know more of their history and we will identify with them to a considerable degree.

Thus the characters in a television program/series that lasts a long time become, so to speak, a part of us; their lives merge with our lives. And the situations in which they become involved take on a significance for the regular viewer that they do not have for the casual viewer. This leads, I suggest, to an inevitable humanization and rounding of the characters, especially in a medium like television, where facial expressions and other signifying systems reveal character so tellingly. It might be argued that regular viewers of a series like *Cheers* see more in a given episode than casual viewers do, though in the pilot episode I'm discussing, all viewers start on an equal footing.

From a semiotic perspective, stereotyping involves the use of conventional and easily understood signifiers and codes as well as easily perceived oppositions. This instant decoding is necessary because television programs don't have a great deal of time to develop characters, and must rely on commonly understood attitudes and beliefs about types of people and their motivations. Stereotyping may also be connected to the inability of some audience members to decode more complex characterizations in texts.

There are some folktale/fairy-tale elements in this episode, and it does not strain credulity too far to suggest that *Cheers* is, though highly camouflaged and modernized, a fairy tale. (We also find that there are fairy-tale elements in many of our important modern story forms: science fiction, detective stories, and westerns). There is a good reason for this. Fairy tales play an important role in our development as children and, it might be asserted, in our adult lives as well. As Bruno Bettelheim explained in *The Uses of Enchantment* (1976:5-6):

> Through the centuries (if not millennia) during which, in their retelling, fairy tales became ever more refined, they came to convey at the same time overt and covert meanings—came to speak simultaneously to all levels of the human personality. communicating in a manner which reaches the uneducated mind of the child as well as the sophisticated adult. In the psychoanalytic model of the human personality, fairy tales carry important messages to the conscious, the preconscious, and the unconscious mind, on whatever level each is functioning at the time. By dealing with universal human problems, particularly those which preoccupy the child's mind, these stories speak to his budding ego and encourage its development. While at the same time relieving preconscious and unconscious pressures. As the stories unfold, they give conscious credence and body to id pressures and show ways to satisfy them that are in line with ego and superego requirements.

When I suggest, then, that there are fairy-tale elements in *Cheers* I am not trying to diminish its significance but to do just the opposite. If *Cheers* is a kind of adult fairy tale, so much the better for it.

The pilot episode involved Diane's initiation into a different world, into the "real" world of working-class people who drink in bars. She has several moments of recognition—when she finds out that she has been jilted and when she realizes what kind of work for which she is best suited.

She is a beauty who finds herself with a "beast" (magnificent pagan), a "princess" who finds herself with an innkeeper in a quasi-medieval city, Boston. The princess has been ditched by her would-be prince; this kind of thing happens all the time in fairy tales.

Cheers was one of the most successful television programs in recent years. Shelley Long left it after the 1986-1987 season. Her descent from English classes to the working classes lasted many years and provided a great deal of first-class comedy. (Comparative literature professors from Boston University—and perhaps from other universities—may not have been amused.)

Conclusion

Professor Saussure's semiotic analysis of a text such as *Cheers* focuses on how meaning is generated and conveyed, and thus on such matters as signs and codes, binary oppositions, and sequential structures. The text functions as a figure against the ground of American culture and the figure reflects (though not always in perfectly accurate ways) the ground, just as the ground helps audiences interpret the figure A text such as *Cheers* is extremely complex and could yield a semiological analysis of even greater length. The lighting, the pacing, the dialogue, the costuming, the blocking, the facial expressions of the characters, the music, the sound—all lend themselves to semiotic analysis because they all function as semiotic signs (and, in particular, signifiers). I have offered a semiotic quick study of *Cheers* in an attempt to show this kind of a study of a text, in this case, the pilot episode of the show might be done. There's plenty of room at the *Cheers* bar, professor Saussure would tell us, for other interpretations of this episode and other episodes.

The first episode of "Cheers' aired on September 30, 1982, on NBC and was 30 minutes in length. The cast was Shelly Long as Diane Chambers, Ted Danson as Sam Malone, Rhea Penman as Carla Tortelli. John Retzenberg as Cliff, George Wend: as Norm, and Nicholas Colosante as Coach.

References

Bettellheim, Bruno. *The Uses of Enchantment* (New York: Knopf. 1976). 5-6.

Culler, Jonathan. *Structuralist Poetics: Structuralism, Linguistics and the Study of Literature* (Ithaca, NY: Cornell University Press, 1975), 4.

Dundes, Alan. "Introduction" in Vladimir Propp. *Morphology of the Folk Tale*, 2nd ed, (Austin: University of Texas Press, 1973). xiv-xv.

Eco, Umberto. "Towards a Semiotic Inquiry into the Television Message," *Working Papers in Cultural Studies* 3 (Autumn 1972): 115.

Lévi-Strauss, Claude. *Structural Anthropology* (Garden City, NY: Doubleday. 1967).

Saussure, Ferdinand de. *Course in General Linguistics* (New York: McGraw-Hill. 1966), 117.

Winick, Charles. *The New People: Desexualization in American Life* (New York: Pegasus, 1968), p. 169.

The range of topics that are used in humorous communication is very wide, and seems to be limited 'only by the number of things there are in the world for us to discuss' (Allen, cited in MacHovec, 1988, p. 11). However, some topics are used as joking material more often than others. Driessen (2004) lists six prominent domains of joking across the world – language, sex and gender, politics, ethnicity, religion, and age. Although we do not have empirical tools to judge if these topics are indeed the most salient joking topics in the world (or even in a specific country), most of them fall in line with the topics that have been studied most extensively by humor researchers in the last century. The six humor topics mentioned by Driessen (2004), as well as other humor topics, can be divided into two categories entitled 'globally oriented' and 'locally oriented.' This division follows a basic tension that characterizes humorous communication: On the one hand, humor is a universal phenomenon, which has accompanied human society from its very beginnings (Boyd, 2004); On the other hand, humor is culture-dependent as it relies on the symbols, stereotypes and codes specific to the place and time of its creation and reception (Boskin, 1997).

Limor Shifman, "Humor in the Age of Digital Reproduction: Continuity and Change in Internet-Based Comic Texts."
International Journal of Communication 1 (2007), 187-209

Chapter 5

Laugh, and the World Laughs with You:
A Global Perspective on Humor

In the United States, there is a popular maxim that goes "Laugh and the world laughs with you; cry and you cry alone." This maxim is an adaptation of lines from Ella Wheeler Wilcox's poem "Solitude" which reads "Laugh and the world laughs with you; weep and you weep alone." In America, we don't use the word "weep" very much, so we tend to use the adaptation and substitute the word "cry." "Weep" sounds too morbid, too traumatic, too refined, too feminine.

This maxim is connected with the notion that it is better to be cheerful and put on a happy face than to tell everyone about your troubles. There are two assertions made in this maxim about laughing and crying. Are they both correct? Is either of them correct? Is neither of them correct?

Though there are two claims made in the maxim, there are, actually, four possibilities that suggest themselves:

1. Laugh and the world laughs with you.

2. Laugh and the world doesn't laugh with you.

3. Cry and you cry alone.

4. Cry and you don't cry alone.

There may be more. We could juxtapose things and say "Laugh and the world cries with you, cry and you laugh alone," or "Cry and the world laughs with you, laugh and you cry alone," but these statements are nonsensical. Or so it seems.

Statement number one suggests that laughter is, among other things, contagious and implies that there are certain examples of humor or maybe kinds of humor that everyone can appreciate. It asserts that, like certain facial expressions, some humor is universal. Statement number two suggests that humor, or, more precisely, some humor may not strike people everywhere as funny, due to matters such as national character, socio-economic class differences, educational levels, and so on. Statement three, "cry and you cry alone," in the hooked-up global village, doesn't seem to be true, for the most part. But some people, after having received "Dear John" or "Dear Jane" letters, may cry alone...for a while, at least. Until they call their therapist, a friend, or another romance possibility or go looking for love on the Internet.

Statement number four, "cry and you don't cry alone," seems to be true. The various tidal waves, hurricanes, earthquakes, floods and other disasters that took place in 2005 elicited widespread outpourings of help, suggesting that in many situations when people cry, they no longer cry alone. People all over the world empathize with victims of hurricanes, tidal waves, earthquakes, recipients of "Dear John" letters, and other terrible things.

Laugh and the World Laughs with You

Let me suggest that while people in different countries with different values and belief systems may not find a given example of humor, such as a particular joke, funny, everyone laughs at joke texts that utilize certain fundamental techniques of humor to elicit comic or mirthful laughter. Let me make an even bolder statement. I would add that we've been laughing at humorous texts that use certain techniques throughout history. And if you look at Greek and Roman comedies, Shakespeare's comedies, and modern theatre of the absurd comedies such as Ionesco's *The Bald Soprano*, to take a few examples, you find that the playwrights used the same techniques of humor.

I am arguing, then, that the techniques of humor are universal and more or less timeless. They have been used everywhere and over the centuries to generate mirthful laughter.

On National Styles of Humor

There's widespread agreement that different countries have what we generally describe as different senses of humor. Many years ago, when I was in graduate school, I was a teaching assistant during a summer course on humor for students who came from all over the world. One day I brought some *New Yorker* cartoons that I thought were very funny and showed them to a group of Japanese students taking the course. None of them cracked a smile. They had a different idea about what subjects were suitable for humor and what kinds of texts were amusing. One of the cartoons involved ridiculing mothers-in-law and I was told that in Japanese culture that was not considered proper.

I would suggest, though, that if you were to take some examples of Japanese humor, you would find that while certain subjects may be off-limits (or were off-limits then, before the global village and the Internet united us all) the creators of humorous texts that amuse Japanese people, use certain techniques that people everywhere might find amusing. That is, it is the selection or patterns of techniques that humorists use that may be distinctive from one country to another. Thus there would certain patterns or matrixes of techniques that are popular in France and other distinctive selections of techniques that are popular in Germany, and so on, ad infinitum. And these patterns may be under attack by our global mass media, and our films and television shows, in particular, moving people all over the world in similar directions in terms of what makes people laugh.

Jokes from Different Parts of the World

To test my hypothesis that some techniques are universal or global, I sent off some E-mail requests to friends in different parts of the world for jokes from their countries. I received any number of responses from people who told me they would be sending me jokes but who never did. This, in itself, can be construed as humorous. It is number 14 in my typology of techniques of humor: disappointment (or defeated expectations), a very commonly used technique. On the other hand, I continually get jokes from friends who know I love jokes and I was able to use some of them.

Let me offer some of the jokes I received. I asked for jokes told by people in a given country about other people in their country, hoping that doing so would lead me to obtain "typical" jokes. The question I wished to answer was—will any of these jokes be ones that my typology doesn't cover? I've already said I believe my typology covers all humor so I'm knocking off a straw man, but by using jokes from some different countries I can demonstrate, I hope, that my claims about techniques being universal are not overdone. Claiming that techniques are universal and have been used through history (at least in the West) is an example, perhaps, of grandiosity—and this, too, is covered in my typology: number 15, exaggeration and maybe number 17, facetiousness!

An Iranian Joke: The Often Married Virgin

A pretty young woman was married five times but she was still a virgin. "My first husband was a Turk, who said I don't touch my own honor; my second was a Qazvini who was interested only in anal intercourse; my third was an Isfahani who said that he didn't don't want to open the seal; the fourth was from Lor who always missed the right spot, and the last was President Khatami, who said beautiful words but did nothing.

As my informant explained, "in Iran, Turks are known to be stupid and very backward, Qazvinis are known as perverts, Isfahani's are infamous for being misers, Lors are known to be simple, and reformers and educated Iranians are used to criticize and mock President Khatami for being too compromising with hardliners." This is a variant of a joke I've seen on an Internet site devoted to

Jewish jokes and is probably found, with different variations, in many countries. The joke uses stereotypes of the way people from different cities in Iran or countries (Turkey) behave and also offers a mild insult to the president of Iran.

An American Joke: The Often Married Virgin (Jewish Variant)

A middle-aged man and woman meet and fall in love and decide to get married. On their wedding night, they settle into the bridal suite at their hotel and the woman says to her new groom, "Please be gentle with me. I'm still a virgin."
The startled groom says "How can you still be a virgin? You've been married three times. "Well, you see it was this way she replies. My first husband was a psychiatrist and all he ever wanted to do was talk about it. My second husband was a gynecologist and all he ever wanted to do was look at it. And my third husband was a stamp collector and all he ever wanted to do was... God how I miss him."
(This joke comes from a website on Jewish humor).

It would seem that jokes with this theme of the virgin who has been married many times are found in numerous countries. The Iranian version is based on stereotypes of the sexual practices of Iranians from different cities or areas in Iran and the Jewish joke is based on stereotypes about occupations.

A Vietnamese Joke

Two Vietnamese students are riding their bikes across a college campus in Hanoi when one asks his friend "where did you get that beautiful bike?"
His friend replies, "I was walking along a street in Hanoi when a beautiful woman rode up to me on her bike. She threw the bike on the ground, took off her clothes and said: "Take anything you want!" The first Vietnamese man said, "Great choice. The clothes probably wouldn't have fit you."

The humor in this joke comes from stereotypes about sexual relations in Vietnam. The man with the bike was more concerned with material possessions than with having sex with a beautiful woman. There are jokes in many cultures with the same theme as this one. The punch line also is interesting and plays with the reader since the first rider suggested it was a good choice. One would think taking the bike was a good choice instead of having sex but the friend replies because the woman's clothes wouldn't have fit the rider who took the woman's bike. There is an element of disappointment in this joke in the reply of the friend.

An English Joke: Three Men in a Bar

An Irishman an Englishman and a Scotsman were sitting in a bar in Sydney. "The view is fantastic, the beer excellent, and the food exceptional but said the Scotsman. I still prefer the pubs back home. Why in Glasgow there's a little bar called McTavish's. Now the landlord there goes out of his way for the locals so much that when you buy 4 drinks he'll buy the 5th drink for you."

"Well." said the Englishman "At my local, the Red Lion, barmen there will buy you your 3rd drink after you buy the first 2." "Ahhh that's nothin'," said the Irishman "Back home in Dublin there's Ryan's Bar. Now the moment you set foot in the place they'll buy you a drink, then another, all the drinks you like. Then when you've had enough drink they'll take you upstairs and give you a passionate night to remember; all on the house." The Englishman and Scotsman immediately pour scorn on the Irishman's claims. He swears every word is true. "Well," said the Englishman "Did this actually happen to you?"

"Not me personally, no," said the Irishman, "But it did happen to my sister! "

What techniques are operating in this text? The fact that we have an Irishman, an Englishman, and a Scotsman as the main characters in the joke suggests that technique number 43, stereotyping, is an important component of the joke.

They are comparing what happens in bars in their countries, so technique number 12, comparison is at work. The punch line, about "taking you upstairs and giving you a passionate night to remember" being something done to the Irishman's sister, not the Irishman, involves technique number 18, exposure, for what they were doing at the bar was getting the Irishman's sister drunk and then exploiting her sexually. If you press hard, you might find some other techniques at work in this joke, as well. Perhaps 45, unmasking? It's quite common, I should point out, to find several different techniques at work in a joke and other forms of humor.

If we were to write a "formula" for this joke, based on the techniques of humor at play in it, we would get:

43	stereotyping
12	comparisons
18	exposure
(45?)	unmasking

Let me now turn to a Japanese joke.

A Japanese Joke: The Two Late Workers

Two workers were late for work one day and their boss summoned them to his office. "Why were you late today?" he asked. "I was dreaming that I was working so hard for the company that I didn't want to wake up and prevent myself from doing the extra work I was doing," said the first one. "Very fine," said the boss. "Even in your dreams you think of working hard for the company. And what about you?" the boss asked the second man. "I was helping him," said the second man.

This joke alludes to the propensity of Japanese workers to overwork and spend a great deal of their time, both on and off the job, involved with their work. In the joke, the basic mechanism involves an escape from embarrassment, technique number 16. The second worker latches on to the attempt the first worker makes. They have both made a mistake, technique number 29, in coming to work late and are trying to escape the consequences of having done so. There may be an element of ridicule, technique number 36, involved here, since coming to work late is not, generally speaking, a serious matter—except in a culture that puts too much emphasis on work.

The formula for this joke is:

16	embarrassment (escape from)
29	mistake
36	ridicule

A joke like this would not be seen as funny in cultures where people are routinely late for appointments.

An Israeli Joke: Doctor and Patient

An eight-year-old girl comes home from school in Jerusalem and tells her mother, "One of the boys in my class asked me today to play

"doctor and patient" with him." "Oh, no!" says the mother. "What did you do?"
" Nothing," says the girl. "He let me wait for half an hour and then said that without form number 17, he can't do anything."

This joke seems to be about sexuality—little boys and girls playing doctor—but it turns out to be a satirical comment about the Israeli medical system. So the dominant technique in this joke is number 39, satire. It ridicules the bureaucratic nature of the Israeli health system. There is also the matter of defeated expectations, technique number 14 since when we read the joke we expect it to have some kind of sexual content to it.

This joke would have the formula:

39	satire
14	disappointment and defeated expectations

It is a relatively simple joke and would probably be seen as funnier by Israelis than by others, though I think people everywhere can recognize bureaucracies of all kinds in all nations and find their dependence of red tape and other such things humorous, especially when it interferes with the kind of "doctor and patient" sex play that we expect to find in jokes about children.

An Argentinean Joke: The Size of His Penis

An Argentinian is questioned by an immigration agent.
"Your name?"
"Antonio Petraglia."
"Age?"
"32 years old."
"Single or married?
"Single."
"Sex?"
"Enormous, really enormous!"

This joke was one of many sent by an Argentinean informant. It is based on technique number 30, misunderstanding. Antonio Petraglia thinks the immigration agent is asking about the size of his genitals, not his gender. The joke also pokes fun at the Argentinean tendency to be boastful, so technique 43 is at work. There are many variations on this joke. In America, when it is told, the punch line is often something like "As often as I can get it," or "right here? I'm game if you are."

The "formula" for this joke is

> 30   misunderstanding
>
> 43   stereotypes

Misunderstanding is a verbal phenomenon and is different from a mistake, which I see as based on faulty logic and errors of that kind.

Conclusions

On this basis of this brief survey, which has jokes from several different countries, we can see that jokes (and by extension other humorous texts) generate mirthful laughter, weak smiles, side-splitting laughter or various other kinds of responses because there are techniques that are operating in them that strike people as funny. I do not pretend to know why people laugh. Why we laugh is a subject that has occupied our best minds from Aristotle's time to the present. Freud has written a wonderful book on jokes, full of Jewish jokes. Many philosophers, psychologists, sociologists and other kinds of scholars have dealt with the matter, from Aristotle's time to the present.

My argument is that while I cannot be certain why we laugh, I have a pretty good notion of what it is that makes us laugh. Humor which uses techniques based on logic, identity and action is the easiest for people all over the world to grasp. Humor based on language—on allusions, definitions, facetiousness, puns and wordplay and that kind of thing—is most difficult for people all over the world to grasp, though it may be amusing to locals and others who may know the language and be familiar with the culture. And globally speaking, humor in countries using idiomatic language and cultural allusions is most difficult for people in other countries to get. Humor that involves sexuality and other such matters (including problems with sexuality) tends to be universal and similar subjects that all human beings experience (dealing with children, wives, girlfriends, boyfriends, mothers-in-law, teachers and professors, politicians) are probably most easily appreciated on a global level. The moral of this exercise is that it seems to be the case that we cry locally and laugh globally!

Note: I would like to thank Peter Couch (English Joke), Limor Shifman (Israeli joke), Ehsan Shahghasemi (Iranian joke), and Beatriz Sznaider (Argentinean joke) for providing texts for my use.

Figure 6.1. Visual Puns Drawings

Concave

Vaticon

Fils du Con

Condorcet

Visual Puns Drawings by the Author

Chapter 6

The Triple Threat:

Arthur as a Writer, Artist, and Secret Agent

or Humor and the Creative Process

In 1954, I was admitted to two different departments at the University of Iowa: I could have worked on an MFA in art or an MA in journalism. Since my brother, Jason, was an artist and since I was drawn more to the literary life, I chose to get an MA in journalism. The University of Iowa also had a great creative writing program and I took advantage of that and took courses in the Writers Workshop with Marguerite Young, a distinguished writer from New York.

I ended up as a writer who illustrated his books and did many illustrations for the *Journal of Communication* and other publications, on the side. This essay explores my experiences as a cartoonist and illustrator. I've been fortunate enough to publish books with many companies whose editors allowed me to use as many of my drawings as I wanted. I also did some book covers for my books and, at times, for books by other writers and publishers.

The Secret Agent

For more than a dozen years I received a large envelope from the editors of *The Journal of Communication* with Xeroxes of the first pages of some articles and book reviews that would be appearing in the next issue of the journal. I drew countless comic illustrations to accompany the articles and reviews and mailed them back to the editors of the journal.

My problem was drawing something that readers of the journal might find amusing and which was connected, as closely as possible, to the article or book review that I was asked to illustrate. Some articles were extremely technical or on very abstract subjects and I was unable to come up with an amusing drawing.

Over the years, my style of drawing, what we might call my "line," became a very fluid and simple one, perhaps even a minimalist one. I draw quickly and directly, generally without a preliminary pencil drawing. One reason I can make my drawings is that I've been illustrating my journals since 1954 and over the years, my line has evolved. It is now much smoother than it was in my earlier years. In some cases, I also make use of written language in my drawings but I rely, for the most part, on conventional representations that most people recognize.

Some people don't like my style of drawing. For example, one reviewer of *Seeing is Believing,* my book on visual communication, criticized my drawings as simple, rough and careless, and suggested that I be required to make more "finished" drawings for any future edition that might be contemplated.

I work by making many, many drawings and letting the editors choose which ones they like best. Thus, at times, when I was illustrating *The Journal of Communication,* I would send six or eight different drawings for the same article or book review and let the editors could choose which one or ones they liked best. In some cases, a drawing I sent for one article or review was used in another one that was on a related subject. And some drawings I sent were held over and used in later issues.

My drawing cartoons for the *Journal of Communication* was the result of a chance event. I wrote an article in the *Journal of Communication* about my work as an analyst of popular culture, "The Secret Agent," and illustrated it with a drawing I did of myself as a secret agent. It appeared in the Spring, 1974 issue of the journal.

George Gerbner, the editor of the journal, asked me to write an article on my work on popular culture. I sent him a long, scholarly essay, and he cut most of it out, keeping only the last section, "The Secret Agent," in which I likened myself to a secret agent investigating all the "secrets" I found in popular culture. I drew a caricature of myself as a secret agent, and that drawing ultimately led to my becoming an unpaid illustrator for the journal.

Figure 6.2. Secret Agent

Secret Agent, Journal of Communication, Spring 1974, p. 71

I did another caricature of myself, based on my interest in semiotics, as a Superhero, "Decoder Man," which I've used over the years.

Figure 6.3. Decoder Man Caricature

Decoder Man Caricature

I generally use my self-caricatures to illustrate my "About the Author" pages in my books, along with photos of myself and sometimes my "Artist, Writer, Secret Agent" embossed image. These pages contain information about my educational background, areas of interest and related matters.

Figure 6.4. Media Criticism Self-Caricature

Generic Drawing on Media

At times, I did what I call a "generic drawing" which could be used to illustrate all articles on a given subject. In my "It's a Rare Medium that's Well Done" drawing (also a self-caricature) I play around with different ways of cooking steak. And, for an article, "A Process Model of Humor Judgment," I did a face laughing (and the teeth spelling HAHA) that is about humor in general but doesn't really deal with the specific topic. Some topics are so abstract or complex that it is very difficult to figure out what images might be used to illustrate them. How might one illustrate the concepts "process" and "humor judgment"? In such cases, a drawing about humor, in general, does the job. Or, one might, if enough space was available, use a series of frames to show the development of humor judgment.

Over the years I did (always unpaid) illustrations for several journals over the years--*Human Behavior, The Army Times* and a small Spanish magazine, *The Guidepost,* and I've illustrated my books and books by other authors. In one of my books, *Signs in Contemporary Culture,* a book I wrote on semiotics, I did spot drawings at the beginnings of each chapter. In this book, I used a technique that I've adopted recently--using a rectangular black background to highlight the drawings.

Figure 6.5. Sample Page from Semiotics Book

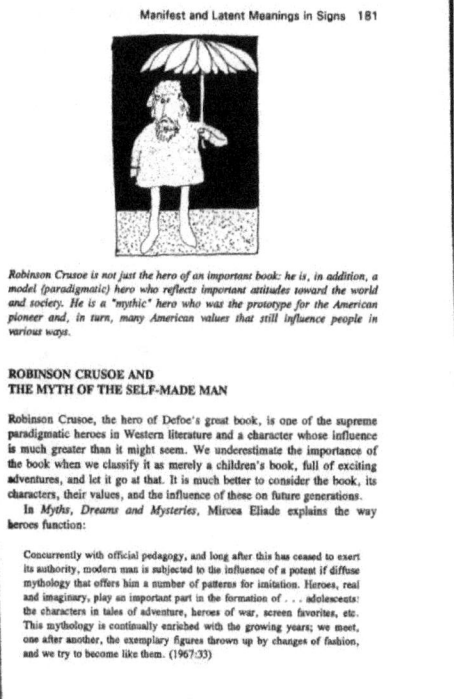

Manifest and Latent Meanings in Signs   181

Robinson Crusoe is not just the hero of an important book: he is, in addition, a model (paradigmatic) hero who reflects important attitudes toward the world and society. He is a "mythic" hero who was the prototype for the American pioneer and, in turn, many American values that still influence people in various ways.

**ROBINSON CRUSOE AND
THE MYTH OF THE SELF-MADE MAN**

Robinson Crusoe, the hero of Defoe's great book, is one of the supreme paradigmatic heroes in Western literature and a character whose influence is much greater than it might seem. We underestimate the importance of the book when we classify it as merely a children's book, full of exciting adventures, and let it go at that. It is much better to consider the book, its characters, their values, and the influence of these on future generations.

In *Myths, Dreams and Mysteries*, Mircea Eliade explains the way heroes function:

> Concurrently with official pedagogy, and long after this has ceased to exert its authority, modern man is subjected to the influence of a potent if diffuse mythology that offers him a number of patterns for imitation. Heroes, real and imaginary, play an important part in the formation of . . . adolescents: the characters in tales of adventure, heroes of war, screen favorites, etc. This mythology is continually enriched with the growing years; we meet, one after another, the exemplary figures thrown up by changes of fashion, and we try to become like them. (1967:33)

Robinson Crusoe Drawing

This is an example of how I used my illustrations in my book on semiotics, *Signs in Contemporary Culture*. These illustrations help make the book more visually attractive. The Robinson Crusoe drawing is based upon a description of Crusoe in the book. Here is another drawing from the book.

Figure 6.6. Back Background Drawing

William Shakespeare

Many years ago, I got the idea of drawing visual puns on the term "CON" and eventually I came up with a series of 60 drawings using the term. Thus, for example, my drawing for the term "content" shows a CON in a tent, and my drawing for the term "condom" shows a striped condom. I used the conventional cartoon representation of CONS as people in striped clothing.

Figure 6.7. Cons Drawings

Content

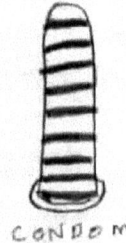

Condom

Lincoln

Con on the Cob

More Cons Drawings by the Author

When you illustrate a book, things are a bit different from illustrating articles. With books, you have a general topic and various chapters that deal with aspects of that topic. Sometimes, in such cases, you have to stretch a great deal to come up with a suitable drawing. For the cover of a book *New Communication Technologies in Politics*, I had to suggest how new technologies were affecting the decision-making process and drew a person's head split open with someone at a computer feeding information into the brain.

Figure 6.8. Drawing from Cover of Book of New Technologies

Advertisers convincing people to buy things.

You have to take advantage of background knowledge in audiences in making illustrations, but sometimes the connections may be a bit distant or too strained for people. In this drawing, used on the cover of my book *Dictionary of Advertising and Marketing Concepts* (Routledge), I think everyone can understand what is going on.

Search and Discovery: Using The 45 Techniques of Humor

My illustrations reflect my sense of play, my sense of the absurd, and my habit of playing with sounds and language. The theory of comic illustration is relatively simple--find some visual signifiers and symbols that people will understand and find amusing and that connect, somehow, to the article or review or book being illustrated. It is finding the right images and allowing readers to make the connections I want them to make that is the problem.

When I am drawing cartoons, I do not think consciously about what techniques I'm using. I use exaggeration, wordplay, caricature, facetiousness, absurdity and so on. I just "search" for a drawing. But all of my drawings use one or more of these techniques. And, I would suggest, all cartoonists and humorous illustrators use visual manifestations of the techniques listed in my chart in their work, though they may not be conscious of doing so. The creative process is not a mechanical one in which a comic illustrator might say "I've not used stereotypes for a while. Maybe I'll try it?"

I believe that what happens is that after years of drawing illustrations, artists get a sense of what might work (or what worked for others) and start playing around to see what they can come up with. This involves using material stored in one's unconscious, to a certain degree.

When I played around, looking for something to use in making an illustration. Ideas more or less bubbled to the surface that I didn't know I had (or didn't have, but somehow came to mind), so drawing comic illustrations is a process of search and discovery in which ideas for illustrations lead to other ideas and from this creative ferment, curious little ink scratches on paper--drawings-- that others will be able to understand in an instant (or in semiotic jargon, decode) and, one hopes, find amusing, emerge.

Wittgenstein said that a philosophy book could be written consisting of nothing but jokes: these would be based on fallacies, category mistakes, and other confusions about the logic of different concepts and arguments. We can even read certain humorous works not intended as philosophy books, such as Lewis Carroll's *Alice in Wonderland* and *Through the Looking Glass* and find many philosophical lessons.

John Morreall, *The Philosophy of Laughter and Humor*

Chapter 7

How Humor Heals:
An Anatomical Perspective

The notion that humor is something that heals is now generally well recognized. Norman Cousins' book, *Anatomy of an Illness as Perceived by the Patient* spread the news of humor's healing powers to the general public. But well before Cousins came along, many others had been doing research and writing about the healing power of humor.

A Bio/Psycho/Social/Cultural Perspective on the Effects of Humor

Thus, the indefatigable William Fry, the notorious chimp tickler, had explained in an address given to the American Orthopsychiatric Association in Washington D.C. as early as 1979 that:

> Mirthful laughter has a scientifically demonstrable exercise impact on several body systems. Muscles are activated; heart rate is increased; respiration is amplified, with an increase in oxygen exchange--all similar to the desirable effects of athletic exercise. Stress is antagonized by humor in both its mental or emotional aspects and its physical aspect. Emotional tension, contributing to stress, is lowered through the cathartic effects of humor. Mirthful laughter is followed by a state of compensatory physical relations, diminishing physical tension.

Fry has made numerous other contributions dealing with the relation of humor and health, and a considerable number of other scholars have done so, as well.

I don't think it is necessary, then, to argue that humor is generally held to help people, in several different ways. I will suggest, in this essay, that exploring how humor "heals" should take a bio/psycho/social/cultural perspective. I will be dealing, then, with the biological, the psychological, the social, and the cultural aspects of humor as they relate to health. These can be correlated with responses of the body (in the biological area) and kinds of communication (in other areas):

Table 7.1. Bio/Psycho/Social/Cultural Areas of Humor

Area	Kind of Communication
Biological	Internal: Physical Responses by body
Psychological	Intrapersonal: Internal dialogues, etc.
Social	Interpersonal: Relations with Others
Cultural	Coded: Learned Methods of Coping

Humor and the Bio/Pyscho/Social/Cultural Perspective

I will deal with these four areas in my analysis of how humor heals, but first, a radical proposal.

A Radical Proposal: It's the Techniques That Do the Work

I have suggested in several works that there are 45 techniques, which used in various permutations and combinations, generate humor in humorous texts: jokes, cartoons, comic strips, plays, movies--you name it. These techniques are the engines that drive the car of comedy and humor and it is these techniques, not the subjects of humor, which are the crucial matter in understanding how humor heals.

What I will suggest is that it is these techniques, in themselves, and separated from the content of jokes, riddles, random comments that evoke laughter--or any other form of humor--are what helps us when we experience mirthful laughter. It is the techniques, often working in combination, behind the message or content aspect of the humor, that do the work.

Humor at the Psychological or Intrapersonal Level

I have already covered the biological aspects of humor. We have seen that mirthful laughter has an immediate physical effect on several systems in the body and there is ample evidence that mirthful laughter stimulates the production of endorphins and has other immediate physical benefits. At the biological level, we have a kind of visceral or neuro-physical communication as the body responds, immediately, to the stimuli generated by humor and laughter.

At the intrapersonal level, when we laugh at ourselves (so to speak), humor helps us recognize that there is an element of absurdity in life, helps us recognize the negative consequences of being overly serious about ourselves and helps us deal with the internal dialogue we often carry on in our heads that often causes problems for us. Many jokes and other humorous texts can be thought of as being similar to the stories that some Hindu medicine healers make up to help patients deal with their problems.

According to Bruno Bettelheim, who discusses this matter in his book *The Uses of Enchantment*, these medicine men create a story which gives form to the problems the person suffers from and by contemplating this story, the afflicted person can understand the impasses he or she is suffering from and ways these problems might be resolved. There is a big difference between being given some abstract information about a problem a person is suffering from and creating a narrative in which this problem is dramatized and ways the problem may be dealt with are suggested.

In one of Matt Groening's strips in *Life in Hell*, ("Parents Out of Control") he has a character, a kid, offer a monologue on the various horrendous things parents often do to their children. The kid says:

> They can really screw up your mind because they're the only parents you know. So you think this is the way the world is, but it isn't. And you end up growing up all weird and damaged and unhappy.

Groening is offering a lecture, actually, in cartoon form, on the problems that people face growing up in so-called dysfunctional families. His zany character and his non-idealized picture of families has, I would suggest, a considerable value to many people who can recognize that they, too, might have had a "childhood in hell," and can laugh at Groening's characters--and then, recognizing that they are like countless others, at themselves. We have here the techniques of analogy and exaggeration at work. Misery, we have been told, likes company--and so, it would seem, do children from dysfunctional families, and others who suffer from one affliction or another.

They recognize that they are not alone.

The Social or Interpersonal Level of Humor

Let me move on, now, to the next level of analysis--the social or interpersonal level, when there are interactions between individuals that are of consequence. Consider the following joke.

Tried it Once and Didn't Like it

Smith is in his club and he's alone, except for one other person. Smith asks the person, "can I buy you a drink?" "No," says the person. "I tried it once and didn't like it." "Oh," says Smith. "Well, would you like to shoot some pool with me?" "No," says the man. "I tried it once and didn't like it. Besides, my son is coming soon." "Your only son, I presume," says Smith.

The man in this joke is rigid--he has the same answer to all of Smith's inquiries. "Tried it once and didn't like it." Thus, the punch line, "Your only son" picks up on this and shows the futility of rigidity. This joke, like a story made up by our Hindu healer for a person who suffers from rigidity and perhaps a mild form of obsessive-compulsive behavior has something to teach us--even though we might not recognize we are learning anything.

Rigidity, over-literalness, and other similar forms of behavior are then ridiculed and one is led to see, in the events that take place in the joke, of the folly of these kinds of behavior. To function in society, and get along with others, we need to be flexible and able to adjust to various problems and complicated situations that come our way. In dramatic comedies, jokes, and other forms of humor, we often have rigid, monomaniacal types who are the butts of the humor: misers, gluttons, dirty old men and women, and so on.

We find many jokes, cartoons and comics deal with problems people face at the interpersonal level--focusing attention on relations between men and women, workers and bosses, parents and children, and so on. And sometimes, we have humor that has a direct socio-political dimension, as we find in many episodes of *Doonesbury*.

How Humor Heals at the Cultural Level

We are now at the final level of analysis, the cultural level--in which humor functions as a kind of coding that pervades a given cultural group or sub-cultural group of some kind. Culture is defined in many different ways, but the anthropological view of culture, which is the one I am concerned with here, generally suggests that culture deals with ways of living that are passed on from one generation to another. Culture involves notions of what is good and bad, what is beautiful and ugly, what is sacred and profane, and how to relate to others and function in society. (Anthropologists have offered more than a hundred different definitions of culture, but they all deal with these topics and see culture as a kind of coding or set of rules for living.)

On the cultural or perhaps sub-cultural level, Jewish humor is worth considering. There are two strains of Jewish humor: that which comes from the shtetls and Eastern-European Jewish life and more contemporary Jewish humor, stemming from the experience of Jews in modern societies. In the shtetls, the Jews were generally poor, were constantly persecuted (suffered from pogroms and other forms of anti-Semitism), but though they lived precariously, on the thin margin of survival, their humor radiates with warmth.

Jewish humor, as I understand it, is humor told by Jews that deals with Jewish beliefs, institutions, cultural practices, historical experiences, and related matters. This humor, in its Eastern European form, involves a remarkable collection of eccentric types and zanies--schlemiels, schlimazels, schnorrers, schadkens and so on--who developed as a consequence of the harsh conditions under which everyone lived and who were accepted as part of life in the shtetls. Jewish humor helped the Jews in the shtetls survive; it was a valuable adaptive coping technique. It kept them alert, it taught them how to laugh at themselves and helped diffuse the anxiety that they experienced.

On Techniques of Humor and Their Salutory Functions

Let me suggest some of the more common techniques of humor used by Jews in Eastern Europe (and in contemporary countries as well) that are connected to their marginality and relative powerlessness. Jews were required to use techniques that were not too overtly hostile and whose aggression could not be easily recognized.

In many cases, we find the Jews using "victim humor" which can be thought of as aggression or "insult humor" that is turned against the teller. But the use of this victim humor is not an exercise in masochism but a subtle and indirect way of attacking enemies. Freud said that he could think of no people who made fun of themselves more than the Jews, but this "making fun" of oneself was not a matter of self-hate at all. It was a defensive form of aggression against others who were more powerful. Let me offer an example.

I'll Take Ten

God comes down to the Assyrians and says "I have a commandment I'd `like to give you." What is it asks the Assyrians? "Thou shall not commit adultery!" says God. "No thanks, " says the Assyrians. So then God comes down to the Babylonians and says "I have a commandment I'd like to give you." "What is this commandment?" ask the Egyptians. "Thou shall not commit adultery!" says God. "No way!" said the Egyptians. So God comes to Moses and says "I have a commandment I'd like to give you!" "How much does it cost?" asks Moses. "Nothing!" says God. "Then I'll have ten!" says Moses.

This joke seems to deal with the stereotype of Jewish cheapness. Moses doesn't ask what the commandment is but how much it costs. But in reality or on a more profound level, it could be argued, the joke deals with the rejection of God and his commandments by others. And the stereotype of Jewish cheapness (ironic in that the Jews are amongst the most generous contributors to charity) must be seen against the background of poverty and deprivation that was the lot of most Jews in the shtetls and small communities in Eastern Europe.

Let us consider, then, some of the basic techniques of humor Jews use in their humor, keeping in mind their relative powerlessness and social marginality. In America, we must remember, approximately 98 out of every 100 people are NOT Jewish.

Table 7.2. Techniques of Jewish Humor and Their Functions

Technique of Humor	Benefits: Shows that
Absurdity	Life is full of illogicalities, crazy things
Accidents	People make mistakes all the time
Allusions	Others screw up, too
Exposure	People do lots of stupid things
Mistakes	Life is a comedy of errors
Misunderstanding	People often get confused about things
Rigidity	Fixations and obsessiveness are self-defeating.

Jewish humor, I would suggest, functioned as a means of transcendence for the Jews in the shtetls and also helped give the Jews a stronger sense of identity.

Conclusions

Humor, we see, functions on many different levels and has many positive effects. At the biological level, it provides exercise and stimulates the production of endorphins. At the psychological or intra-psychic level, it helps us cope with our internal dialogues and lessen the severity of our feelings of guilt and anxiety. At the social or interpersonal level, it facilitates our relations with others (sometimes distracting us when we are angry or confusing communication so that people who should be antagonistic towards one another don't recognize they should be hostile). And at the cultural level, humor helps members of various ethnic groups and sub-cultures maintain their identity and cope with problems connected to their marginality and status.

Humorists are, it could be said, unacknowledged therapists of mankind and humor has obvious and impressive therapeutic value--at every level we find it. Humor helps us avoid obsessive behavior, it relieves us of feelings of guilt, it fosters creativity, and it purges us of violent emotions. Conrad Hyers points out in *Zen and the Comic Spirit* that the Zen masters acted like clowns and made use of humor in their teaching for hundreds of years. Our humorists and comedians can be thought of, then, as secularized versions of the Zen masters who, without recognizing what they are doing (and often without our recognizing what they are doing) help heal us, and perhaps also help us learn how to heal ourselves.

Numerous running jokes and themes develop throughout the series. Chief among them are the class and familial conflicts among Frasier, Niles, and Martin. The two sons, who possess "fine" tastes, "intellectual" interests and rather high opinions of themselves, frequently clash with their more blue-collar, down-to-earth father. A running theme, particularly in the early seasons, is Frasier's and Martin's difficulty in reaching an accommodation with each other and in sharing an apartment. Despite being similar in personality, interests, and sensibilities, the relationship between Frasier and Niles is no less turbulent. Despite their mutual love of sherry, opera and ballet, they are constantly victims of intense sibling rivalry, their jealousy of each other and petty attempts at one-upmanship (which frequently result in chaos) drive many of the plots. Other developing storylines include Niles' growing love for Daphne (of which she remains unaware in the early seasons, despite its increasingly obvious nature) and the breakdown of his marriage to the never-seen Maris (a take-off from its parent series, "Cheers," in which Norm's wife, Vera, was often talked about--and even heard--but never seen), Frasier's search for love in his own life, and the various attempts of the two brothers to gain acceptance into Seattle's cultural elite. Structurally, many episodes center around misunderstandings or elaborate lies which multiple characters are forced to "play along" with in order to conceal the truth. *Frasier* also featured many "once-a-year" plot devices, such as an appearance by Frederick, Lilith, or Bebe. Season finales sometimes took the form of a "two-part" special that was concluded as the series premiere the following season.

Wikipedia *Frasier*

Chapter 8

Mediated Mirth:
A Study of "The Good Son," the Pilot
Episode of *Frasier*

Frasier was, for many years, one of the most popular sitcoms on television. Its pilot episode was brilliant and many other episodes were of equally high quality, though in its last years after Niles Crane married Daphne Moon, it deteriorated considerably. But it's hard to maintain quality in a sitcom that runs for many years. Even *Seinfeld* lost some of its luster in its final two or three years. (NOTE: I will italicize the situation comedy *Frasier* but print the name of the character Frasier in Roman script. I will put the titles of episodes in quotes, as in "The Good Son.")

This analysis will deal with the techniques of humor and with the role the television medium plays in helping generate laughter in mass-mediated humorous texts, with a focus on "The Good Son." Of course, it is impossible to separate the visual and auditory aspects from the dialogue and plot, so I will have something to say about all these matters.

The Characters

The creators of *Frasier* were very fortunate in putting together a collection of characters whose complicated relationships generated much of the comedy. The lead character, Frasier Crane, a radio psychiatrist, can be described as an effete snob who spends much of his time chasing after women and not succeeding with them, for one reason or another. His brother Niles Crane, also a psychiatrist, is an even more of a snob, a prissy man who always wipes off chairs with his handkerchief before he sits in them. He is married to Maris, a character who is never seen but is frequently talked about—invariably in negative terms. Niles, whose relationship to Maris is always troubling, spent many years on the show madly in love with Daphne Moon, a somewhat wacky English woman who was the physical therapist for Martin, the father of the Crane brothers. Martin Crane is a blue-collar type, who stands for everything—in the way of taste in cultural matters—that the Crane brothers find repugnant. He is also very sarcastic and rather bitter. He lives with Frasier because he was shot in the hip and cannot manage on his own. Martin has a dog, Eddie, his best friend, who stares at Frasier all the time and is used, with great effect, to generate comedy. The last major character, Roz Doyle, is a man-crazy woman who, like Frasier, is also frustrated in her attempts to find a meaningful relationship with a member of the opposite sex. She is an attractive woman, but that doesn't seem to help her satisfactorily assuage her sexual needs. She has many dates and affairs, but things never work out.

Since Frasier is a radio psychiatrist, there are many other characters who become involved in various episodes when they call in for advice. This enables the creators and writers of the show to insert all kinds of weirdos when it is convenient for them. There are also other characters in the radio station where Frasier has his show and other characters who show up for one reason or another, in the various episodes.

All of the major characters tend to be fixated on one thing or another; in the best tradition of comedy, they are monomaniacs. Comedy often deals with character types who, because of their monomania and fixations, become the butt of much comedy. We find the following "fixations" in the main characters:

Frasier:	fixated on finding a beautiful, cultivated woman
Niles:	fixated on Daphne
Daphne:	wacky and unpredictable working-class Brit. Is "psychic."
Eddie:	stares at Frasier all the time
Roz:	fixated on finding sexual partners
Martin:	loves blue-collar pleasures and putting down snotty sons.

A great deal of the comedy involves the interplay between the opposing character types, with their various fixations, obsessions, passions, and personality quirks. We have the following relationships that can be used to create comedy:

Frasier and Niles	Niles and Martin	Brothers and Martin
Frasier and Martin	Eddie and Frasier	Brothers and Daphne
Frasier and Roz	Niles and Daphne	Frasier and callers
Guest Weirdos		

Other characters are introduced in various shows to further complicate matters. For example, in one show there is a doppelganger who Daphne picks up in a bar who is about the same height as Niles and has similar behaviors (he, too, uses his handkerchief to wipe off chairs, etc.) In many shows, women who Frasier fancies are introduced, but he always manages, one way or another, to screw things up and fails to have a satisfactory relationship with any of them.

We must recognize that what might be called comedic (that is, not serious) conflict is an essential element in all situation comedies, just as conflict—of one kind or another--is basic to all narratives. Situation comedies are about problems that have to be solved in which there is conflict about how to solve the problem and conflict among the characters about matters related to the conflict. This conflict creates tensions that the stories resolve. Comedies are full of clowns, fools, zanies, oddballs, and eccentrics, who get "slapped" in each adventure, but live on to be "slapped" again. In tragedies, the dead bodies of the heroes and villains litter the stage. The problem to be solved in "The Good Son" involves finding a place for Martin to stay, since he cannot stay on his own.

Performance Qualities

One of the reasons the show was so successful was that, in addition to the wonderful writing (from a team of more than a dozen full-time writers, plus other script doctors and specialists), the performers were so superb. One secret of comedy is that the characters, who are frequently involved in inane situations, play it straight and don't give the audience a sense that they realize that they are being fools. By chance, the creators of *Frasier* were able to assemble a team of marvelous actors and actresses. Their facial expressions, their body language, the way they speak their lines, their remarkable comedic timing, all helped make the show a success. All of this was captured by the television camera.

It is not easy to create a situation comedy, and the same team that created *Frasier*—David Angell, Peter Casey, and David Lee—flopped miserably when they created a new show called *Encore, Encore*. It can only be described as terrible. The show had a wonderful cast, but the characters were not interesting and they didn't have relationships that could be mined for good comedy. I don't think it lasted more than two or three weeks and it was really painful to watch the show. You wondered how a team as talented as the one that created *Frasier* could create *Encore, Encore*.

Frasier had just a few sets: the radio station where Frasier worked, his apartment, full of expensive furniture, and Café Nervosa, the coffee shop where everyone repairs for coffee and chatter and much of the action takes place. The last show during the first season, "My Coffee With Niles," takes place entirely in the café. (In that episode there is a suggestion that Niles is gay, and many critics have suggested that there is a homosexual subtext in the series.) Other sets were used from time to time, but the three main sets dominated the show. In the pilot script, "The Good Son," we find Martin bringing his blue-collar "working-class" vibrating lounging chair into Frasier's tastefully coordinated apartment, setting up a visual contrast. He sets the chair, which is ugly and all beat up, right opposite the television set, so he can drink beer and watch ball games on television. His behavior is just the opposite of everything that Frasier and Niles stand for. Their tastes run to antiques, opera, and French restaurants. That chair became a signifier of the ongoing clash of wills, temperaments, and tastes in the show.

On the Techniques of Humor

I argue that one or more of my 45 techniques of humor can be found in jokes, dialogue in plays, scenes in novels and texts of all kinds. We find these techniques operating in everything from Roman comedies to situation comedies such as *Frasier*. My thesis is that comedy writers haven't articulated these techniques and aren't necessarily conscious of them, but that they pick up these techniques as they develop their expertise in comedy writing. I also believe that these techniques are universal and can be found in texts from all countries and in all times. This assertion has not been accepted by some critics, who argue that my 45 techniques can be reduced to a much smaller number.

Consider the technique of facetiousness. In order for a remark to be seen as facetious, we have to consider the way characters saying something facetious act, their facial expression, and the tone of voice they use. In some cases, such as imitation and impersonation, there is a visual component to this kind of humor that plays an important role in its success. In other cases, what is said generates images in our minds that help create the humor.

The Medium of Television and Humor

When dealing with an audio-visual medium like television, it is useful to consider how television achieves its effects. It uses sound, lighting, camera work, and editing techniques. I discuss some of the more important elements of these matters below.

SHOT	DEFINITION	USE FOR HUMOR
Reaction shot	reaction of character	response to comic event or statement
Close-Up	face only	intensifies reactions
Medium shot	most of body	shows expressions and body language
Full shot	whole body	shows expressions and body language
Long shot	setting and characters	context: sets up humor, shows responses

Frasier is shot very simply, mostly with medium shots of characters and often medium two-shots and three-shots of characters. Close-ups are avoided since they suggest too much intensity.

CAMERA	DEFINITION	USE FOR HUMOR
Cut	switch to new image	shows relationships, creates excitement
Wipe	imaged wiped offscreen	ends scene
Dolly In	camera moves in	inspection. Anticipates humor
Dolly Out	camera moves out	response of characters to humor
Zoom In	lens moves in	inspection. Anticipates humor
Zoom Out	lens moves out	response of characters to humor

There are subtle differences between dollying in and out and zooming in and out, but they are not important for our purposes. Dollying and zooming are used to alert audiences to something comedically important happening—a bit of repartee, an embarrassing coincidence, and so on. Situation comedies are brightly lit, a technique knows as "flat" lighting. Comedies avoid chiaroscuro lighting, with strong lights and darks, that people connect with very strong emotions. Most situation comedies have laugh tracks, which are meant to key audiences to something characters do or say that is (supposedly) humorous. Laughter is contagious and laugh tracks are meant to stimulate and intensify laughter in audiences who are, presumably, too stupid to laugh at the right times. Situation comedies make use of sound effects but not music.

In "The Good Son," the camera work is very simple. There are lots of cuts between two-shots and three shots, and occasionally, to establish context (as in the Café Nervosa), long shots. It is not a heavily edited text. When I watched it, and I've viewed it many times, I was amazed at how simple it was presented. *Frasier* did make use of one innovation: announcing scene changes with white text on black boards. This technique is similar to using sub-heads in written works and facilitates the matter of informing audiences of changes in scenes.

Comedic Techniques in "The Good Son."

"The Good Son" was the pilot episode of *Frasier*, and did a beautiful job of introducing audiences to the main characters and establishing the relationships that existed among them. We must remember that while characters are talking with one another, the director of the show is employing various kinds of shots and editing techniques to intensify the comedic aspects of the dialogue. We must also keep in mind the facial expressions of the characters, their body language, and their timing, which play an important part in generating humor. Let me deal with just a few of the many techniques employed in "The Good Son."

Mistakes (Number 29 in my typology)

Mistakes, which are things people do (in contrast to misunderstandings, which are verbal and involve communication failures) are one of the most important techniques found in comedy. Mistakes, of course, are only funny if there is a comic "play frame" around them. At the end of a scene, Frasier asks Roz, his producer, how his first show went.

> *He gets up and enters Roz's booth. She is busy with administrative stuff.*

> FRASIER

> It was a good show, wasn't it?

> ROZ

> [*tears him a piece of notepaper*] Here, your brother called.

> FRASIER

> Roz, in the trade we call that "avoidance." Don't change the subject, tell me what you think.

> ROZ
> [*points at her console*] Did I ever tell you what this little button does?

> FRASIER

> I'm not a piece of Lalique. I can handle criticism.

> How was I today?

> ROZ

> Let's see. You dropped two commercials, you left a total of 28 seconds of dead air, you scrambled the station's call letters, you spilled yogurt on the control board and you kept referring to Jerry with the identity crisis as "Jeff."

This bit of dialogue was accompanied by certain actions and facial expressions from Roz and reaction shots of Frasier that heightened its comic aspects. Most of the shots were two-shots—that is, shots with two people in them. Frasier is revealed, almost immediately in the first episode, as something of a klutz, a bumbler prone to making mistakes. There is an element of irony in that Frasier, technically speaking a comedic fool, is a somewhat pompous and stuffy radio psychiatrist, who earns his living advising people who call him about their problems.

It is useful to think of situation comedies as 22-minute plays in which some kind of a problem presents itself and has to be solved. The other eight minutes are devoted to commercials, which force the situation comedy to structure itself in certain ways so that audiences will be kept curious about how some scene will be resolved when its time for the various commercial breaks. In "The Good Son," Frasier and Niles have to figure out what to do with their father. The matter is complicated because they don't get along with their father and have different tastes. Frasier's mention of Lalique shows him to be somewhat precious, and Niles is even worse. They consider sending their father to a nursing home but eventually since he can't live with Niles and Maris, they decide to have him move in with Frasier. He accepts this resolution but is not very happy about it.

Exposure and Revelation of Character. (Number 18 in my typology)

We are introduced to Niles when he tells this story about his "fight" with Yoshi, his Japanese gardener. We must keep in mind his facial expressions and body language as he recounts this tale.

> NILES
> So I said the gardener, "Yoshi, I do not need a
> Zen garden in my backyard…If I want to rake gravel
> every 10 minutes to maintain my inner harmony, I'll move
> to Yokahama."…Well, this offends him so he starts pulling
> up Maris' prized camellias by the handful. I couldn't stand
> that so marched right into the morning room and locked the door until
> he cooled down.

Niles reveals a great deal about himself in this passage. He is, we see, a wimp— who "wins" his battle with his gardener by retreating ("I marched right into") to his morning room and locking the door. There is an element of reversal and defeated expectations here, for instead of doing something positive, Niles avoids conflict. When Niles speaks these lines, he does so with a sense of assurance in his manhood and ability to deal with problems, that makes the lines even funnier.

Insults and Repartee (Numbers 25 and 33 in my typology)

Insults, of one kind or another, are probably the most commonly used techniques found in comedy. An insult by itself, of course, is not funny. But in a situation comedy, in which there is a play frame established that says "these insults are not serious," they have a comedic quality to them. And they have the added virtue of often leading to a repartee, a counter-insult, so to speak, which means they have a double payoff. Consider the following bit of dialogue between Niles and Frasier:

> NILES
> You know what I think about pop psychiatry.
> FRASIER
> I know what you think about everything. When was the last time
> you had an unexpressed thought?

Niles, we see, thinks the "pop psychology" that Frasier practices as a radio psychiatrist is a waste of time. This is an indirect insult—one which Frasier answers with his comment about knowing what Niles thinks about everything. This suggests that Niles is both talkative and highly opinionated. The insults here are veiled and indirect, but audiences still can recognize their import—both from the dialogue and from the facial expressions, body language and editing techniques used in this scene.

   Another example of insults occurs when Niles and Frasier and discussing Maris, Niles' wife.

> NILES
> Dad doesn't get along with Maris.
> FRASIER
> Who does?
> NILES
> I thought you liked my Maris.
> FRASIER
> I do. I like her from a distance. You know,
> the way you like the sun. Maris is like the sun...
> except without the warmth.

Here Frasier is insulting someone who is not present and insults her by informing us that nobody gets along with Maris and by comparing her to the sun, saying she's like the sun--but without its warmth. This suggests she's a very cold individual and it is best to keep one's distance. When Frasier says "I do," we can see from his facial expression that he really doesn't. Invidious comparisons are a very powerful means of insult. When Frasier spoke this line, his somewhat bemused facial expression gave the line more resonance.

Comedies Are Often Serious, but Not Solemn

Although *Frasier* could be, at its best moments, absolutely hilarious, it also had an undercurrent of poignancy about it, and many of the episodes were both funny but also touching. This was expressed by the dialogue and the way the plot got resolved, but also by the body language and facial expressions of the performers and the way the director used the camera and editing techniques to generate the desired response. In television comedies, writers and directors work backward: they determine the effects they want and then figure out how to use language, lighting, camera shots, editing techniques and anything else to obtain these effects.

Frasier was a great success for many years until it faltered during its last few years. It was immensely popular not only because it was funny but also, I would suggest because it was often both touching and profound.

An Appendix on the Show

Frasier was on television for eleven years during which 264 episodes were filmed. The show won 31 Emmys. Peter Casey, one of the creators of the show, based the character Martin on Casey's father, who was a police officer for more than thirty years. Casey is a graduate of the Broadcast & Electronic Communication Arts Department at San Francisco State University, where I taught from 1965 until 2003. I offered a course on writing situation comedies for many years and one year Peter Casey was kind enough to come up to San Francisco and give a three-hour presentation to my students on how *Frasier* was created and the problems involved in writing and producing a situation comedy. He also was kind enough to give me copies of the six revisions and rewrites of a script that were generated for one episode, showing how much change there is as scripts evolve. Eddie was played by two dogs: Enzo (a rather unfriendly and unresponsive dog) and his son Moose (who was very friendly and loved to be petted). In keeping with one of the major plotlines in the show, Enzo and his son Moose did not get along and had to be kept separated. My discussion of the techniques of humor in "The Good Son" draws upon "Frasier: a 20th Century Fool" in my book *The Agent in the Agency* but was rewritten for this essay.

The main performers in the show were:

Frasier Crane	Kelsey Grammer (who played the role in *Cheers*)
Niles Crane	David Hyde Pierce
Martin Crane	John Mahoney
Daphne Moon/Crane	Jane Leeves
Roz Doyle	Perry Gilpin

References

Berger, Arthur Asa. 1970. *Li'l Abner: A Study in American Satire* New York: Twayne.

Berger, Arthur Asa. 1975. *The TV-Guided American.* New York: Walker & Co.

Berger, Arthur Asa. 1993. *An Anatomy of Humor* New Brunswick, NJ: Transaction Publishers.

Berger, Arthur Asa. 1995. *Blind Men & Elephants: Perspectives on Humor* New Brunswick, NJ: Transaction Publishers.

Berger, Arthur Asa. 1997. *The Art of Comedy Writing* New Brunswick, NJ: Transaction Publishers

Berger, Arthur Asa. 1997. *The Genius of the Jewish Joke* Northdale, NJ: Jason Aronson

Berger, Arthur Asa. 2003. *The Agent in the Agency: Media, Popular Culture and Everyday Life in America* Cresskill, NJ: Hampton Press.

Smith, Evan S. 1999. *Writing Television Sitcoms,* New York, NY: Perigee

A glance at some of the common features of comic lines, behavior or situations reveals a close analogy between comic techniques and Zen techniques, as well as the serviceability for comic techniques in Zen: irrationality, contradiction, incongruity, absurdity, irrelevancy, triviality, nonsense, distortion, abruptness, shock, sudden twist, reversal or overturning. In both comedy and Zen, one is prevented from drawing a purely intellectual conclusion at the end of an argument and therefore entering the abstractness and deceptiveness of a pseudo-appropriation of truth.

Conrad Hyers. *Zen and the Comic Spirit.*

It appears that the most crucial element in the dissemination and use of ethnic humor is the perceived ambiguity of the speaker's intentions and motives by those who are its target. There is an increased collective sensitivity on the part of minority ethnic groups to their being made the butt of humor because of their past experiences of social, cultural, and political oppression, and of public ridicule and humiliation.

Mahaved L. Apte, "Ethnic Humor Versus 'Sense of Humor'"

There is a kind of warmth and loving quality to much of the Old-World Jewish humor. It was the humor of a truly oppressed people who, despite their poverty and problems, made room, somehow, for all the bizarre types (schnorrers, schlamtzls, schlemiels, etc.) who populated their world. There was an openness and warmth and good-naturedness reflected in the jokes and the stories about the people in the shtetls that was remarkable, considering the difficult situation in which Old-World Jews found themselves.

Arthur Asa Berger, *An Anatomy of Humor*

Chapter 9

Notes on Jewish Humor

1. What are the unique features of Jewish Jokes?

Let me begin by saying something about what it is that makes humor Jewish. I offer a Jewish Joke and then an explanation of what it is that is Jewish about the joke.

Cohen Remembers

Cohen showed up at synagogue one Saturday and the rabbi almost fell down when he saw him. Cohen had never been seen in a synagogue in his life. After Services, the rabbi caught Cohen and said: "Mr. Cohen, I am so glad you decided to come here. What made you come?" Cohen said, "I got to be honest with you, Rabbi, a while back, I misplaced my favorite hat and I really, really love that hat. I know that Levy had one just like mine and I knew that Levy came to Services every Saturday. I also knew that Levy takes off his hat during Services and he leaves it in the back of the Shul. So, I was going to leave after the SHMAH and steal Levi's hat." The rabbi said: "Well, Cohen, I notice that you didn't steal Levy's hat. What changed your mind? Cohen said, "Well after I heard your sermon on the Ten Commandments, I decided that I didn't need to steal Levy's hat." The rabbi gave Cohen a big smile and said: "After I talked about 'Thou Shalt Not Steal' you decided you would rather do without your hat than burn in Hell, right?" Cohen shook his head and said: "No, Rabbi, after you talked about 'Thou Shalt Not Commit Adultery' I remembered where I left it."

2. What Makes a Joke Jewish?

What is it about this joke that makes it a "Jewish" joke? A joke is defined as a short narrative, meant to amuse and evoke mirthful laughter, with a punch line. This joke is Jewish for the following reasons:

1. It deals with Jews and their relationships with one another.
2. It deals with Jewish religious teachings—in this case, the ten commandments.

3. It uses Jewish terms, such as "shul."

4. It reflects the degree to which many Jews are estranged from their religion and its teachings. Cohen, let us remember, had never been to a synagogue before in his life. The punch line, which reveals that he is an adulterer, shows the degree to which he has become like many other Americans, with little regard for the teachings of the ten commandments and Jewish ethical standards.

5. It is told by Jews about Jewish culture, values, beliefs, and behaviors.

This joke is more easily comprehended by Jews and by Gentiles who may have relatively little familiarity with Judaism. They can probably figure out that a shul is a synagogue. The fact that Jews have been so prominent as comedians in America has led to the fact that many Yiddish terms are now commonly used by Jews and Gentiles alike—terms such as "schlepped," "maven," and "schmuck."

There are jokes told about Jews by non-Jews that often are hostile and rely on ugly and unreal stereotypes of Jews. An example of this would be the JAP: Jewish American Princess joke cycle.

A Jewish Princess Makes Dinner

What does a JAP make for dinner?
Reservations (at restaurants).

It is ironic. The JAM: Jewish American Mother lives to cook and to feed her children while the JAP avoids cooking and is obsessed with buying clothes and participating in American consumer culture.

3. Are there any taboo subjects in Jewish humor?

The joke, we must understand one particular *form* of humor; there are many other forms of humor, such as riddles, fables, comic verse, witticisms, and puns. Although many comedians no longer tell jokes, Jewish jokes are still alive and well on the Internet, as I will show shortly. I would argue that there are no subjects that jokes and other kinds of humor don't deal with. There are no taboo subjects in humor, in general, and Jewish humor, in particular. Humor covers every aspect of our lives. There are even concentration camp Jewish jokes. Humor is also used by Jews as a means of calling attention to problems in societies, reflecting a cultural belief in social justice and a desire to make sure that they are protected by the governments of the countries in which they live.

I would suggest that humor functions, among other things, as a coping mechanism for Jewish people, who find themselves as marginal in most countries. If Jews make up two percent of the population in the United States, it means that ninety-eight percent of the people in the United States are not Jewish. In most countries, the number of Jews is much smaller.

4. Techniques Used in Jewish Humor

Many techniques of humor are available to comedians such as allusions, insults, ridicule, exaggeration, parody, and facetiousness. We didn't find jokes in *Seinfeld*, the most popular situation comedy in America for many years, though at the beginning of the series Seinfeld had a couple of minutes before each show in which he did stand-up comedy. But even that was mostly observational humor. And Jackie Mason, one of the most durable and important Jewish comedians of recent years didn't tell jokes, as a rule. Instead, he relied on stereotypes, exaggeration and other techniques to "insult" both Jews and non-Jews. I would describe him as an equal-opportunity ridiculer and insulter. We might be able to use my charts (page xii) to discuss whether there are any typical techniques used in Jewish jokes to find out something about the Jewish sense of humor. That is, are there certain techniques that are typically found in Jewish humor that we do not find commonly used in humor by other religious, ethnic, racial or socio-economic groups?

Jewish humor is alive and thriving in America, even though Jews no longer dominate the field of comedy the way they did in the Thirties and Forties when something like eighty percent of the comedians were Jewish. In recent years we find more African-American and Hispanic comedians coming into the spotlight, but this doesn't mean that Jewish comedians and comedy writers are still not over-represented in show business or that Jewish humor isn't all-pervasive in American society.

You must keep in mind the marginality of the Jews in America (and everywhere else, except Israel). There are approximately 300 million people living in America and about six million Jews who live here. That means that Jews now represent about two percent of the population. Strange as it may seem to many people, some 98 out of every 100 Americans are *not* Jewish, or as Humpty Dumpty would put it "un-Jewish.". Forty or fifty years ago, the figure would be 97 out of every 100 Americans aren't Jewish.

5. The Internet and Jewish Humor

Probably one of the most important development in recent years for the dissemination of Jewish humor, all over the world now, is the Internet. Thirty years ago, many Americans got their Jewish humor from comedians like Myron Cohen, who performed regularly on the Ed Sullivan Show. Now, with the development of the Internet, Jewish jokes and other kinds of Jewish humor (and now Jewish humor, as well) are spread quickly, and too large numbers of people. by E-mail. Twenty years ago, I used to get my good Jewish jokes from my brother Jason, an artist, who lived in Boston. He had a friend, a businessman, who got wonderful Jewish jokes from a friend by phone. Jason's friend would phone my brother and tell him the jokes and then my brother would phone me. That system of disseminating Jewish jokes and Jewish humor has changed with the development of the Internet. Jewish jokes and humor are now global in their reach.

Let me offer some examples of Jewish humor that I've received in recent weeks in E-mail messages from friends. What E-mail does is allow Jews to target other Jews (and on some occasions, non-Jews) who it can be assumed will "get" the humor. That is, they have the background and cultural information that enables them to understand the humor is the jokes and other forms of Jewish humor transmitted by E-mail.

6. Jewish Punning and Playing with Language

In my typology on the techniques of humor, making comic definitions are categorized as linguistic humor. Freud had a great deal to say in his book *Jokes and Their Relation to the Unconscious* about the kind of amalgamations found below. They are nothing new.

1. JEWBILATION
Pride in finding out that one's favorite celebrity is Jewish.

2. TORAHFIED
Inability to remember one's lines at one's bar or bat mitzvah.

3. SANTA-SHMANTA
The explanation Jewish children get for why they celebrate Hanukah while the rest of humanity celebrates Christmas

4. MATZILATION
Smashing a piece of matzo to bits while trying to butter it.

5. BUBBEGUM
Candy one's mother gives to her grandchildren that she never gave to her own children.

6. CHUTZPAPA
A father who wakes his wife at 4:00 AM so she can change the baby's diaper.

7. DISORIYENTA
When Aunt Sadie gets lost in a department store and strikes up a conversation with everyone she passes.

8 GOYFER
(n) A Gentile messenger.

9. KISSKA
Smooching at a bar mitzvah and getting the telltale smell of stuffed derma.

10. MEINSTEIN (slang)
"My son, the genius."

11. MISHPOCHAMARKS
The assorted lipstick and make-up stains found on one's face and collar after kissing all one's aunts and cousins at a reception.

12. RE-SHTETLEMENT
(n) Moving from New Jersey to Florida and finding all your old neighbors live in the same condo as you.

13. ROSH HASHANANA
A rock 'n roll band from Brooklyn.

14. YIDENTIFY
To be able to determine true ethnic origins of celebrities even though their names might be St. John, Curtis, Davis, or Taylor.

15. FEELAWFUL
Indigestion from eating Israeli street food.

16. DISKVELLIFIED
(v) To drop out of law school, med school or business as seen through the eyes of parents, grandparents, and Uncle Sid. In extreme cases, simply choosing to major in art history when Irv's son, David, is majoring in biology, is sufficient grounds for diskvellification.

17. KINDERSCHLEP
(n) To transport other kids in your car beside yours.

18. SCHMUCKLUCK
Finding out one's wife became pregnant after one had a vasectomy.

19. OYVAYSCHMEAR
(Slang) What one says when the cream cheese squeezes out of the bagel and falls on your clean pants.

20. JEWDO
(n) A traditional form of self-defense based on talking one's way out of a tight spot.

These comic definitions involve playing with words and making reference to various aspects of the everyday experience of many Jews. As more and more Jews become assimilated and lose touch with their Jewish background, it may be that the humor in these definitions will be lost of future generations of Jews.

My next Internet selection involves parodies of Japanese Haiku poems that have been adapted to Jewish culture and society—mostly involving second generation or older Jews confronting the new American reality of assimilated and non-affiliated Jews.

NEW JEWISH HAIKU PARODIES

Lacking fins or tail
the gefilte fish
swims with great difficulty.
       *****
Hard to tell under the lights.
White Yarmulke or
male-pattern baldness.
       *****
After the warm rain
the sweet smell of camellias.
Did you wipe your feet?
       *****
Her lips near my ear,
Aunt Sadie whispers the name
of her friend's disease.
       *****
Today I am a man.
Tomorrow I will return
to the seventh grade.

*****

Testing the warm milk
on her wrist, she sighs softly.
But her son is 25.

*****

The sparkling blue sea
reminds me to wait an hour
after my sandwich.

*****

Like a bonsai tree,
your terrible posture
at my dinner table.

*****

Beyond Valium,
the peace of knowing one's child
is an internist.

*****

Jews on safari-
map, compass, elephant gun,
hard sucking candies.

*****

The same kimono
the top geishas are wearing:
I got it at Loehmann's.

*****

The shivah visit:
so sorry about your loss.
Now back to my problems.

*****

Mom, please! There is no
need to put that dinner roll
in your pocketbook.

*****

Seven-foot Jews in
the NBA slam-dunking!
My alarm clock rings.

*****

Sorry, I'm not home
to take your call. At the tone
please state your bad news.

*****

Is one Nobel Prize
so much to ask from a child
after all I've done?
     *****

Today, mild shvitzing.
Tomorrow, so hot you'll plotz.
Five-day forecast: feh
     *****

Passover left the door open
for the Prophet Elijah.
Now our cat is gone.
     *****

Yenta. Shmeer. Gevalt.
Shlemiel. Shlimazl. Meshuganah
Oy! To be fluent!
     *****

Quietly murmured
at Saturday services,
Yanks 5, Red Sox 3.
     *****

A lovely nose ring,
excuse me while I put my
head in the oven.

These parodies are all based on making-fun of various aspects of Jewish culture, such as over-protective Jewish mothers, Jewish tendencies in shopping, Jewish rituals such as Bar Mitzvahs, and other Jewish passions and pre-occupations. One of these involves having a son who is a doctor (and one who is an internist is even better), and another deals with wanting to talk about one's problems rather than listen to someone else talking about their grief at a Shivah service, held for people who have just died. The Yenta (a yenta is a busybody) haiku plays with Yiddish language and the haikus about Jewish basketball players and women with rings in their nose deals with the resistance of many older Jews to changes occurring in Jewish culture. The threat to put one's head in an oven and commit suicide is the punch line found in many jokes involving Jewish men and women marrying non-Jews, to the dismay of their parents.

The Nature and Uses of Laughter

Robert Provine, a psychologist who has done important work on laughter, has defined a laugh as follows ("Laughter," *American Scientist,* Vol. 84, Jan-Feb. 1996):

A laugh is characterized by a series of short vowel-like notes(syllables) each about 75 milliseconds long, that are repeated at regular intervals about 210 seconds apart. A specific vowel sound does not define laughter, but similar vowel sounds are typically used for the notes of a given laugh. For example, laughs have the structure of "ha-ha-ha" or "ho-ho-ho" but not "ha-ho-ha-ho."

One interesting thing that Provine found while conducting his research is that "most conversational laughter is not a response to structured attempts at humor, such as jokes or stories. Less than 20 percent of the laughter in our sample was a response to anything resembling a formal effort at humor." What he discovered was that people often laughed at banal remarks such as "Are you sure?" and "It was nice meeting you, too." He found that "mutual playfulness, in-group feeling, and positive emotional tone—not comedy—mark the social settings of most naturally occurring laughs.

Provine is dealing with everyday and conversational humor, which is different from formal attempts by comedians and jokesters to be funny. The Jewish humor by professional performers that I've been writing about—taking the form of jokes and observational humor, are somewhat different from conversational humor. Jews use their humor often in an attempt to deal with groups that are more powerful than they are and often play with stereotypes that non-Jewish populations (such as American White Anglo-Saxon Protestants, that is WASPs, and Catholics) have of Jews.

Jews use them to make fun of non-Jewish populations who do not realize that they are being ridiculed and mocked by the seemingly self-deprecatory Jewish jokes. It's a sense of superiority, not masochism, that is the sub-text of much Jewish humor.

We didn't find jokes in *Seinfeld,* the most popular situation comedy in America for many years, though at the beginning of the series Seinfeld had a couple of minutes before each show in which he did stand-up comedy. But even that was mostly observational humor. And Jackie Mason, one of the most durable and important Jewish comedian of recent years, doesn't tell jokes, as a rule. Instead, he relies on stereotypes, exaggeration and other techniques to "insult" both Jews and non-Jews. I would describe him as an equal-opportunity ridiculer and insulter.

On the Otherness of the Jews

The fact that much Jewish humor ridicules non-Jews, as well as Jews, has led the British sociologist Christie Davies to describe Jewish humor as "balanced." That's because Jews mock themselves and everybody else. As he writes in *The Mirth of Nations* (2002:51):

The Jews have been as successful in inventing jokes about outsiders, enemies, and deserters as about themselves in a way that is not found among the self-deprecating Scots. For this reason I shall speak of the balanced Jewish sense of humor.

He points out that while the Jews have words for non-Jews, namely "goyim," the Scots don't have a word for people who are not Scottish. As he explains, "In Jewish jokes and humor the goyim often have a purely negative identity: *they are what the Jews are not.*" (2002:55, my italics)

As an example of Goyish "otherness" let me quote some "Gentile Jokes" that someone sent me by E-mail.

> A Gentile goes into a clothing store and says, "This is a very fine jacket. How much is it?" The salesman says, "It's $500." The Gentile says, "OK, I'll take it."
> ***
>
> Two Gentiles meet on the street. The first one says, "You own your own business, don't you? How's it going?" The other Gentile says, "Just great! Thanks for asking!"
> ***
>
> Two Gentile mothers meet on the street and start talking about children.
> Gentile mother 1 (said with pride): "My son is a construction worker!"
> Gentile mother 2 (said with more pride): "My son is a truck driver!"
> **
>
> A Gentile man calls his mother and says, "Mother, I know you're expecting me for dinner this evening, but something important has come up and I can't make it." His mother says, "OK."
> **
>
> A Gentile couple goes to a nice restaurant. The man says: "I'll have the steak and a baked potato, and my wife will have the julienned salad with house dressing. We'll both have coffee." The waiter says, "How would you like your steak and salad prepared?"
> The man says, "I'd like the steak medium......the salad is fine as is."
> The waiter says, "Thank you."
> **
>
> A Gentile man calls his elderly mother.
> He asks, "Mom, how are you feeling? Do you need anything?"
> She says, "I'm feeling fine, and I don't need anything. Thanks for calling."

Compare the relationships between sons and mothers in the Gentile jokes with the ones between Jewish sons and their mothers. A classic Jewish joke on this matter shows the difference clearly.

> **A man gets off a train and dials a number.**
> "Hello," says a woman.
> "It's me, mom," he says. "I just got in."
> "Wonderful," says the woman. "Come over right away. I'm making you some of your favorite dishes.'
> "Great," says the man.
> **"I'm making chicken soup and matzoh balls and flanken," says the woman.**
> **"But I don't like chicken soup and I hate flanken. Say, is this 385-2997?"**
> "No," she says. "It's 385-2998."
> "Oh," he says, "Excuse me. I called the wrong number."
> **"Does that mean you're not coming?" asks the Jewish mother.**

I think you can see that these "Gentile" jokes, which were popular in Los Angeles a while back, reflect a much different sensibility than Jewish jokes do.

This matter of "otherness" is important, for it suggests that Jews use the term "goyim" as a means of securing and consolidating their Jewish religious, ethnic and cultural identity. Jews define themselves by being different from others, by being what others "are not.". The Swiss linguist, Ferdinand de Saussure, explained that "in language, there are only differences" and that concepts don't have an innate meaning but gain their meaning by being different from other terms. He wrote in his book *Course in General Linguistics* (1966:117) :

> Concepts are purely differential and defined not by their positive content but negatively by their relations with other terms in the system. Their most precise characteristic is in being what the others are not.

This helps us understand the importance of the insight Davies offered us about the relations between Jews and non-Jews.

Thus, when Jackie Mason complains (but not seriously) that many Jews find his humor "too Jewish," he is suggesting that his humor, in a subtle manner, represents a means of helping Jews maintain their identity in the face of assimilationist pressures. Jews have a very high rate of intermarriage and it may be that Jewish otherness is being diluted or will be destroyed by this process, except, that is, for Orthodox Jews, whose dress and cultural behavior are most significantly "other" to non-Jews, and to some Jews, as well.

Conclusions

The role of the comic "other" is now being taken, to some degree, by African-American and Latino comedians and members of other ethnic minorities in the United States. But these comedians find themselves dealing with an American public whose comic sensibilities have been shaped, in large measure, by Jewish humor. I would suggest that while most professional comedians nowadays, as a rule, don't tell jokes, most ordinary people do. I'm using the word "tell" here to mean via spoken word or, more importantly, by the printed or typed words found in Internet E-mail messages. There are, it turns out, 783,000 websites listed for "Jewish Jokes" on Google. And many people find that when they open their E-mail, some friend (or some web site devoted to sending off Jewish jokes every day or every week) has sent them Jewish jokes and other forms of Jewish humor—such as the comic definitions, jokes and parodies found earlier in this Introduction.

Professional comedians may no longer tell jokes, but the Jewish joke lives—on the Internet and, in its oral form, at Bar and Bat Mitzvahs, parties and other social events where Jews are with other Jews. And that is because, as I explain in *The Genius of the Jewish Joke*, Jewish jokes and Jewish humor are functional and serve a variety of purposes for Jews.

A joke is a play upon form. It brings into relation disparate elements in such a way that one accepted pattern is challenged by the appearance of another which in some way was hidden in the first. I confess that I find Freud's definition of the joke highly satisfactory. The joke is an image of the relaxation of conscious control in favor of the subconscious...The joke merely affords the opportunity for realizing that an accepted pattern has no necessity. Its excitement lies in the suggestion that any particular ordering of experience may be arbitrary and subjective. It is frivolous in that it produces no real alternative, only an exhilarating sense of freedom from form in general....

My hypothesis is that a joke is seen and allowed when it offers a symbolic pattern of a social pattern occurring at the same time. As I see it, all jokes are expressive of the social situations in which they occur. The one social condition necessary for a joke to be enjoyed is that the social group in which it is received should develop the formal characteristics of a "told" joke: that is, a dominant pattern of relations is challenged by another. If there is no joke in the social structure, no other joking can occur.

Mary Douglas. "Jokes" in Mary Douglas, *Implicit Meanings: Essays in Anthropology*. London: Routledge and Kegan Paul. 1975:96, 98.

Chapter 10

Deconstructing a Russian Joke

Throughout the ages, some of our greatest minds, philosophers and thinkers as diverse as Aristotle, Plato, Kant, Hobbes, Schopenhauer, Bergson, and Freud, and I could go on endlessly--have offered a variety of different answers to the question—why do we laugh. My concern is not with why we laugh but what makes us laugh, which is a considerably different question. In this anatomy of a joke, I will deal with comic devices or techniques of comedy found in humorous texts such as jokes (that is, what techniques make us laugh) and what these jokes reveal about the cultural, social and political arrangements in the societies in which they are found. In this investigation, it is Russian society and politics that I deal with.

My list of 45 techniques of humor is, in certain respects, similar to Vladimir Propp's list of functions in *Morphology of the Folktale* (1968) though I had not read Propp when I worked out my list of techniques. They are dealt with in considerable detail in my *An Anatomy of Humor*, Transaction, 1993, which devotes a long 50-page chapter, "A Glossary of the Techniques of Humor: Morphology of the Joke-Tale" to describing and explaining each technique and offering relevant examples. I argue, also, that if one wants to be humorous, it is much better to use the different techniques found in my charts to create one's own humor instead of retelling someone else's material, which is what we do when we tell a joke.

As I explained earlier, a joke is conventionally defined as a short narrative text, meant to amuse, with a punch line. This punch line is a "surprise" and is what generates the humor. This surprise takes the first part of the joke and "opposes" it, we might say, by adding an unexpected element, which comes in the punch line. This punch line generates some kind of meaning or recognition or insight which elicits laughter (when the joke is a good one). We move from a linear narrative or syntagmatic structure with the telling of the first part of a joke to a paradigmatic structure with the punch line, in which there is meaning that is unexpected and which generates a set of simple binary oppositions that can be elicited from the text.

To show how these techniques can be used to deconstruct jokes, let me analyze a wonderful Russian joke. If pushed too far, analyzing a joke (or any other text) with these techniques might end up as overly mechanistic, but some of the techniques, such as allusions (to gaffes that celebrities or politicians have made and that kind of thing) involve social and political or, in more general terms, contextual matters of significance. So we do not anatomize or "kill" humorous texts when we examine the techniques found in them. We cannot help but consider where jokes are told, what they are told about and how the jokes relate to the societies and cultures in which they are told. The techniques are, then, a supplementary tool to understanding jokes and other humorous texts but an important one, since they help us understand how the humor is created. The caller to Radio Erevan generally speaks with a Jewish accent, so we can consider these jokes to have a connection to Jewish humor.

Comrade Gasparow Wins 10,000 Rubles

A caller asks: "Dear Radio Erevan, is it true that Comrade Gasparov won 10,000 rubles in the state lottery?"
Radio Erevan answers: "Yes, it is true! But it was not Comrade Gasparov but Academician Smirnov. And it was not 10,000 rubles but 5,000 rubles. And he didn't win it in the state lottery but lost it gambling."

Let me use my techniques to see how the humor is generated in this text and then analyze it's social and political significance in some detail. There is often a considerable among of variation in specific joke-texts, in terms of names used and that kind of thing, but the example below contains the fundamentals of the joke as I remember it. My informant was a Russian physician visiting the United States who I met at a dinner party.

The most important humorous technique found in this joke is Number 43 in my chart, stereotyping. The Radio Erevan jokes are about Russia and its satellites and about the impact of socialism and communism on the lives of people living in societies dominated by Russia. Stereotypes are metonymic, and, more precisely, based on synecdoche, in which a part is used to stand for the whole or, in ethnic jokes, a small number of people, whether Scots or Poles or Irish or Jews or Russians are taken as representative of all Scots or Poles or Irish or Jews or Russians.

The second most important technique used in this text is number 35, reversal and contradiction. Radio Erevan says "yes, it is true" to the caller but then points out that the caller was mistaken about who was involved in the story and what happened. It is this "yes, it is true!" that is pivotal. It is the beginning of an extended punch line in which every part of the caller's story is reversed. If Radio Erevan had said "No," and then repeated the remainder of the joke, there would be no humor. But the "yes" of Radio Erevan is tied to the way people see it, the

Communist party, and Russian/Eastern-European society. In this text, the material leading up to the punch line is relatively short and the punch-line element is extended.

It might be suggested that this text also is a parody of the kind of double-talk one gets in Communist societies, in which truth, according to some Marxist theorists, is whatever the Party says is true even when the Party often speaks out of both sides of its mouth at the same time. Thus, if the party contradicts itself, both the original assertion and the subsequent contradiction are correct.

Radio Erevan is telling its caller what he wants to hear, namely that he is correct, and then undermines every aspect of the caller's question. The naïve caller is revealing his ignorance, technique 21, another commonly used technique: he's mistaken (technique 29), it turns out, about everything. In addition, there is the technique of revelation in which Radio Erevan inadvertently reveals the inadequacies of Communists societies, where a bureaucracy tells people what they want to hear, "Yes it is true," but undermines them and reveals that they know very little about what is really going on, even though they may think they do.

A polarity is set up in the joke between the caller and Radio Erevan, between truth and falsehood. Radio Erevan says "yes, it is true," to the caller, which is a falsehood since, in reality, the caller is wrong about everything. The caller asks "is it true" and recites a list of things that reveal his ignorance and turn out to be false. This polarity is shown in the following chart.

Table 10.1. Characters in Radio Erevan Joke

CALLER	RADIO EREVAN
asks a question	gives an answer
seeks validation	confirms that questioner is right
is it true?	yes! (but not really)
Comrade Gasparov	Academician Smirnov
won	lost
10,000 rubles	5,000 rubles
state lottery	gambling

Oppositions in Radio Erevan Joke

This joke, I would suggest, reflects the cynicism that many Russians and people in countries living under Russian domination felt about Russian society and the Communist Party and the way it lied to them about so many things and is a humorous but biting indictment of Russian politics and society in the Communist era.

References

Bateson, Gregory. 1972. Steps to an Ecology of Mind. New York: Ballantine Books.

Berger, Arthur Asa. 1974. "Anatomy of the Joke." *Journal of Communication.* Summer, 1976. Vol. 26, No. 3.

Berger, Arthur Asa. (Ed.) "Introduction" to "Humor, the Psyche and Society." *American Behavioral Scientist.* Vol. 3, No. 3, Jan/Feb 1987.

Berger, Arthur Asa. *An Anatomy of Humor.* 1993. New Brunswick, NJ: Transaction Books.

Borges, Jorge Luis. *A Universal History of Infamy.* 1972. New York: Dutton.

Douglas, Mary. *Implicit Meanings.* 1975. London: Routledge & Kegan Paul.

Dundes, Alan. *Cracking Jokes: Studies of Sick Humor Cycles and Stereotypes.* 1987. Berkeley, CA: Ten Speed Press.

Freud, Sigmund. *Jokes and Their Relation to the Unconscious.* Translator: James Strachey. 1963. New York: W.W. Norton.

Fry Jr., William F. *Sweet Madness: A Study of Humor.* 1968. Palo Alto, CA: Pacific Books.

Grotjahn, Martin. *Beyond Laughter: Humor and the Subconscious.* 1966. New York: McGraw-Hill.

Piddington, Ralph. *The Psychology of Laughter.* 1963. New York: Gamut Press.

Powell, Chris and George E.C. Paton, eds. *Humour in Society: Resistance and Control.* 1988. New York: St. Martin's Press.

Propp, Vladimir. *Morphology of the Folktale.* 1968. Austin, Texas: University of Texas Press.

Humor is therefore defined as a social message intended to produce laughter or smiling. As with any social message, it fulfills certain functions, uses special techniques, has a content, and is used in certain situations. These aspects of humor can be understood as relating to the questions of *why* people use humor (its functions), *how* it is transmitted (techniques), *what* it communicates (content), and *where and when* it is communicated (situation). Some of these aspects of humor are universal, characterizing humor everywhere. Others are more influenced by culture.

Avner Ziv. *National Styles of Humor.*
New York: Greenwood Press. 1988.

Chapter 11

Little Britain:

An American Perspective

Little Britain is a cult hit in Britain, where its catchphrases are now part of everyday speech. The DVD of the first year, which is the subject of this analysis, was 'Britain's biggest selling DVD' according to the BBC UK 'Guide to Comedy'. *Little Britain* is a remarkable tour de force of comedic acting by its two writers, Matt Lucas and David Walliams. Thanks to some wonderful wig-makers and make-up artists, they play all the main roles in the show and do so brilliantly.

Little Britain and American Comic Strips

Why is it that when I watched *Little Britain* I kept thinking about how it was similar, in many ways, to certain classic American comics strips such as *Krazy Kat, Li'l Abner, Peanuts* and *Dilbert*? *Little Britain* is a sketch show, made of short segments of varying lengths, each of which is complete in itself. In this respect, it is similar to comic strips such as *Krazy Kat, Li'l Abner, Peanuts, Doonesbury, and Dilbert.* The show is full of grotesques—bizarre comedic types, often with monomaniacal fixations and obsessions of one sort or another, and in this respect, it reminds me of the American comic strips mentioned above and American underground comics, as well. Think, for example, about Ignatz Mouse, the hero of *Krazy Kat,* who spent decades figuring out how to crease Krazy Kat's head with a brick. Or of Charlie Brown, never able to kick a football held by Lucy. Or of the marvelous zanies in *Li'l Abner* such as Fatback Roaringham, who pursued their crazy passions with boundless energy.

Contemporary humorous comic strips can be defined as having continuing characters, a narrative thrust that generally ends each day with a gag or some kind of humorous twist and with dialogue in balloons. As I see *Little Britain*, it is very much like a comic strip, except that it is acted out on television. The same kinds of zanies that populate *Dilbert* can be seen in *Little Britain*; in fact, some of the characters found in *Dilbert* are even more bizarre than those found in *Little Britain.* The show is also close to American underground comics in terms of their extreme characterizations; one thinks of 'Mr. Natural', 'The Fabulous Furry Freak Brothers', and other characters from underground strips that are as bizarre as the characters in 'Little Britain.' But the characters in the

American underground comics are heterosexual unlike many of the characters in *Little Britain*.

The American Comedic Sensibility

I only watched the first year of the show so I can't comment on how it evolved, but watching the first year of *Little Britain* made me think about how different it is from American televised comedy shows. American television humor, in general, isn't as crude, low-brow, and vulgar as *Little Britain* and other low-brow British television shows from the past such as *Benny Hill*. *Little Britain*, in its sketch structure, resembles *Monty Python* and American shows from years ago such as *Laugh-In*. American comedic television is essentially made up of situation comedies, and none of our situation comedies is as imaginative, bold, or as tasteless as *Little Britain*.

When my wife saw the show she was turned off by it and described it as infantile. In a sense, all the characters in the show are like infants, and like children unable to break away from their childish behavior. The title of the show, 'Little Britain' can be taken literally. The humor is also often very low-brow: the way the gardeners trim the hedges in the Dame Sally Markham skits, as penises and breasts, for example, strikes me as both crude and not particularly funny. Americans do not, as a rule, find men dressing up as women hilarious while it would seem British audiences really enjoy that kind of thing. And while we have gays in some of our comedies, we don't have gays like Daffyd, the "committed homosexualist," who takes pride in being the only gay in his small Welsh village, even though he's mistaken about this assertion. Daffyd, like many of the characters in *Little Britain*, refuses to face reality—and this takes on a comic turn since in episode after episode he has to deal with other gays in the village (the barmaids turn out to be lesbians) or gays who come to visit the village for one reason or another. Repetition, with variations, is a basic element in comedy and in the show.

Consider, by way of contrast, the two great American situation comedies of recent years: *Seinfeld* and *Frasier*. Both of those shows also had characters with numerous fixations and obsessions, but the humor in these shows was much more sophisticated than we find in *Little Britain*. Kramer, the weirdo in *Seinfeld* probably comes closest to the kind of characters we find in *Little Britain*, which pushes its characterizations to extreme lengths and seems to revel in bad taste.

Most of the comedy found on contemporary American television either comes from films that are being broadcast or from situation comedies. Shows like "*Little Britain*" are not popular now and earlier comedy shows such as Sid Caesar's "*Show of Shows*," made in the early fifties, no longer are being made. We do have comedy in our late-night shows, which are basically interview shows that star comedians or spoofs of news shows by comedians. In part, situation comedies are popular because they are a formulaic narrative genre, and are, relatively speaking, easier to produce than other genres of comedy shows. It has been said "Death is easy, comedy is hard" and that applies to all kinds of comedy. It is much easier to make people cry than it is to make them laugh. It isn't difficult to make bad or mediocre situation comedies but it is very difficult to make great ones.

Another reason is that the financial payoff from a successful situation comedy is so great that even though most situation comedies fail and many successful ones do not last very long, a great situation comedy such as *Seinfeld* or *Frasier* makes an enormous amount of money, both in terms of the amount of money charged for commercials on these shows and because of the hundreds of millions of dollars to be made on their reruns.

Humorous Techniques in Little Britain.

The show is a satire on British culture and society, as its title suggests—a show about the 'little people' in Britain, the ordinary folk—though a Prime Minister wouldn't, generally speaking, be considered an ordinary or typical British person. Technically speaking, it would seem to be a *Menippean* satire, which Northrop Frye, in his *Anatomy of Criticism*, has described as one that: (1957:224)

> deals less with people as such than with mental attitudes. Pedants, bigots, cranks, parvenus, virtuosi, enthusiasts, rapacious and incompetent professional men of all kinds are handled in terms of their occupational approach to life as distinct from their social behavior.

I would modify Frye's' notion about the occupational approach to life and suggest that this kind of satire has much to say about social behavior—though we could say that the behaviors of the characters in the show are their occupations.

Satire generally attacks the status quo, though sometimes it is used to reinforce power relationships in society. In *Little Britain*, there is a certain ambiguity about who is being ridiculed—the eccentrics and grotesques in the show or the British society that produces them. There seems to be a correlation between class-bound hierarchical societies such as we find in Britain and eccentric behavior. In hierarchical societies, where everyone knows his or her place, it is easy to be an eccentric since you don't have to worry about your status. This isn't the case in egalitarian societies like the United States, though its egalitarian ethos is actually more myth than reality and doesn't adequately recognize the class-based nature of American society. Social mobility is higher in a number of countries than in the United States but the myth of the self-made man and woman still survives. Our aristocracy is based to a considerable degree on achievement, not heredity.

Generally speaking, most of the techniques employed in *Little Britain* come under the category of identity humor. It is a show about people with all kinds of identity problems such as Daffyd, the homophobic "only gay in the village;" Andy Pipkin, who pretends he can't walk so Lou Todd will do all kinds of things for him; Marjorie Dawes, a fat leader of a fat-fighter group who refuses to recognize that she's fat; and Emily Howard, the transvestite, who doesn't seem to be aware that most everyone can see through her.

We see theme and variation in the skits that always end the show, in which the characters are seeking to set a world record of one kind or another, always attempting something absurd and silly and always being frustrated and miscalculating one way or another so their efforts come to naught.

The Dame Sally Markham skits involve caricature and imitation. Caricature traditionally involves comic drawings that exaggerate a person's features, but it can also be used for portraying types of individuals and professions. Dame Sally is a romance novelist who resembles a famous writer who allegedly can dictate three or four different novels at the same time to her secretaries. Dame Sally lies on her sofa, with her lap dog, and dictates novels, but she's always asking how many pages she's written and finding ways to pad her books because she doesn't want to do the work of dictating a complete novel. In one scene, lacking ideas and looking for filler material, Dame Sally turns on the radio and has her faithful secretary type what she hears.

Andy Pipkin and Lou Todd

In the case of Andy Pipkin and Lou Todd, we have "discrepant awareness" operating. This involves a situation in which the members of the audience know something that one of the characters doesn't know—namely that Andy can walk. He often walks, jumps off swimming pool diving platforms and so on, but Lou never sees him doing this. In my typology, discrepant awareness is classified as a form of ignorance. Another example of discrepant awareness would be the scene in which a man at the bar is attracted to "Emily" Howard and offers to buy her a drink. When she goes to the bathroom, he says, to the barkeeper "she's gorgeous." He is shocked and confused a few moments later when he goes to the men's bathroom and finds Emily there.

In addition to the use of discrepant awareness, we also have theme and variation in the Pipkin-Todd skits. We know that Andy will always choose something he won't like, such as a greeting card or a color to paint his room. He always chooses something that Lou knows Andy doesn't like but Andy will insist on getting what he chose. So Lou will buy a greeting card or paint a room the color Andy chose, and then, a second later Lou will change his mind and say "I don't like it" or indicate that he wants something different.

Members of the audience know that Lou will always change his mind and will want something different from what Lou has purchased for him. The variations involve the different things Lou wants to buy or have Lou do for him. Lou is continually being disappointed—he always hopes that just this one time Andy will like what he says he wants, a technique I call "defeated expectations." And, of course, Andy never does. Lou never learns, which is what makes the routines so funny to audiences who are all waiting for the moment when Andy changes his mind.

In a sense, viewers of the show have been "conditioned" to respond to Andy's behavior—a kind of comedic conditioning that is not too far removed from Pavlov's experiments. The use of catchphrases is an important element in this conditioning—analogous to Pavlov's ringing a bell when he fed his dogs. When we hear these catchphrases uttered by the characters in the show, we don't salivate but we laugh.

Identity Humor and the British Psyche

What *Little Britain* relies upon is its audience having a familiarity with the various characters and their obsessions and an appreciation of the way the show satirizes a number of different aspects of British culture such as grammar schools, Prime Ministers, Welsh small-town life, and Scottish hotels. It is the continual repetition of scenarios related to British culture, in which characters act out their obsessions in numerous variations, that generates much of the humor, so the show is probably much funnier to people in Britain than it is to Americans—who probably don't get many of the allusions—and it is also funnier, I would imagine, to those who have watched it over a period of time than it is to someone seeing one episode for the first time. The same applies to American comic strips like *Little Abner, Krazy Kat, Peanuts, Doonesbury* and *Dilbert.* The longer you follow these comics, the funnier the characters become.

Little Britain can be thought of as a "gay" show and one that reflects attitudes (problems?) about sexual identity found in British society. Daffyd is gay, Emily Howard is a transvestite and Sebastian Love (aptly named) has a crush on the Prime Minister. Some critics have suggested that *Frasier* should be considered to be a gay show, but in America, many gay television shows tend to disguise their true nature whereas, in England, that doesn't seem to be the case. Having gays in a show isn't the same thing as having a gay show. Perhaps the attitudes towards sexuality in *Little Britain* are a reflection of the fact that England is much less Puritanical than the United States and much more open about sexuality. Mary Douglas, the social-anthropologist, dealt with the relationship between humor and culture in her book *Implicit Meanings.* She discussed jokes but her insights about humor and society are applicable to the gags in *Little Britain*.

There is an element of the theatre of the absurd in *Little Britain*. Some of the sketches have a touch of Ionesco's *Bald Soprano* in them—in their subversion of logic and language. There's also a bit of *Waiting for Godot*, as well—the endless repetition and meaningless chatter in the show as the characters endlessly wait for a resolution--Godot's arrival.

One problem with extreme characters like the ones we follow in *Little Britain* is that while we find them amusing and we may laugh while we watch the program, I would suggest that we don't identify with them and don't become emotionally involved with any of them. So while the show is, to my mind, brilliant and extremely clever, it is curiously empty and doesn't move me at all. That may be because I'm an American and can't empathize with the characters, but I tend to think it is because the characters are all so one-dimensional and hollow.

That wasn't the case with the best episodes of *Frasier* or *Seinfeld*, for example, where viewers laughed at what went on but also were often moved. We laugh at the zanies in *Little Britain*, but we don't laugh with them. We see them over and over again, so we do get to know them, but they never grow and are very much like comic strip characters that we find amusing but recognize that they aren't 'real.'

Theories of Humor and Little Britain

Aristotle said that comedy involved making people ridiculous, and Lucas and Walliams and their colleagues have certainly done a wonderful job of doing that with their bizarre characters. Aristotle is a proponent of the *superiority* theory of humor, which states that we laugh at others because we feel superior to them. In Britain, which is a class-ridden stratified society, with its Lords, Ladies, Royals and so on, this kind of humor finds a natural home. In an egalitarian society such as America, it would be more difficult for this kind of a show to succeed. How the Americanized version of the show will do when it is shown in the United States is hard to predict.

A second group of humor theorists suggests that it is *incongruity* that is basic to humor—we are amused by incongruous resolutions that we don't expect, such as the punch lines in jokes. Bergson's theory of types would be an example of incongruity theory. He wrote about the mechanical being encrusted upon the living and said that when characters resemble machines and are automaton-like, in that they exhibit "mechanical inelasticity," we have humor. Bergson's notions about comedic types help explain the humor in *Little Britain* which is full of invariant character types and it is their invariability and inability to adapt to different situations that we find amusing.

A third group of humor theorists argues that humor is based upon *masked aggression,* a theory promulgated by Freud and a number of other humor scholars who have adopted his ideas. If you examine the humor in *Little Britain,* you can see that there is a great deal of aggression in the show, such as the way that various kinds of people (gays, cross-dressers) and various professions (the Primer Minister, professors, hotel keepers, psychiatrists) are ridiculed. Psychological studies of comedians reveal that most of them are very hostile, and they deal with their hostility and aggressive feelings by being making people laugh—or trying to do so. And members of the audiences of comedies get rid of their aggressive feelings by laughing at others.

What the creators of *Little Britain* have done, I would suggest, is create a collection (I was tempted to use the term 'bestiary') of bizarre and zany characters who never change. Once the mold is cast, the characters will all play their parts with only mild variations in the events that will transpire. This rigidity is humorous at first, but after a while, it becomes tedious. What Lucas and Walliams haven't done, as I see things, is made their characters human, given them souls.

One facet of the role of the comedian with regard to listeners' expectations of him is that he legitimates a situation whereby, in laughing with him at the stereotypical pattern of his jokes depicting the humour of a morally stressful social situation in real life, e.g. living with a mother-in-law, being discriminated against because of one's race, ethnicity, etc., this distances the listener from or temporary suspends involvement in a real-life situation which clearly would be stressful, intolerable or insufferable for the social actors themselves in reality, especially if they expressed such unvoiced sentiments in non-joke situations in which social tensions exist. Similarly, the comedian articulates and expresses linguistically the moral sentiments, attitudes, opinions, etc. which his listeners perceive as meaningful or recognizable and which they are inhibited by normative conventions from saying or cannot articulate/express so readily or so well. (1988:207)

George E. C. Paton, "The Comedian as Portrayer of Social Morality." in *Humour in Society: Resistance and Control.*

Chapter 12

I Laughed Last, and I Lasted
(But I Took Some Blows Along the Way)

I see myself as essentially a humorist who did his gigs in universities, not comedy clubs. This has caused problems for me with some academicians who take themselves seriously and with many of my students, who didn't know how to take me. I've found that most of the scholars I have met who are outstanding in one way or another have a very good sense of humor. People who have confidence in themselves can enjoy the comedy of life. For example, my friend, the late Aaron Wildavsky, who was a world-class political scientist, had a wonderful sense of humor. The first time we met he told me some wonderful Jewish jokes. We even talked about collaborating on a book on humor before his untimely death and we did work on an article together that was published in *Society* magazine.

The distinguished philosopher Gustav Bergman, with whom I studied at the University of Iowa, once said: "If I had the choice between making a very funny joke, which would cost me the friendship of my best friend, and not telling the joke, I would tell the joke." That statement liberated me and I spent the rest of the semester making puns and other comic statements in his course.

I don't tell jokes, as a rule. (I once wrote an essay titled "How to be funny without telling jokes for people who tell jokes without being funny.") What I do is play with ideas, play with sounds, make puns and sometimes witticisms, and generally clown around—too much for my own good at times, I fear. I come from a family of humorists. My mother told dirty jokes on her death bed. And when I was a child, my father used to tell me stories about the "no-soapie Indians" and liked to draw cartoons. My brother Jason, an artist, was a compulsive punster and after a while became obnoxious and impossible to be with since he was incapable of not punning. He punned in three languages and generally found a way to make a pun on the average of once or twice a minute, or so it seemed. There probably is a medical term for that affliction, but I don't know what it is.

I draw funny illustrations for my books (and books by others, at times) and write articles in which I play with ideas and make wild analogies. This doesn't mean that I'm not serious, but generally speaking, I see the absurdity in life and in the best postmodern tradition, I am, on occasion, a sociological "put-on" artist and ironist.

Some of my students have told me I'm "far out," but I explain to them that, in truth, I'm close to the center of contemporary intellectual thought, and that they are "far in." There's nothing students dislike more than being told they're "far in" or that they are "boring." They seem to think that only they have the right to use that word to dismiss everything that they don't find entertaining. One of my students once asked me if I would hold up my left hand when I was being serious and wanted students to take notes.

One of the secrets of being a humorist is to do comic things but with a straight face, and to offer comic ideas in the guise of solemn social science. I wrote a book, *Bloom's Morning*, with chapters in which I considered matters such as the sexual identity of household appliances—those with the incorporative modality were feminine (most of our appliances) and those with the penetrating modality were masculine (the electronic knife and little else). In short, I was having fun with my analyses which often seemed absurd to many social scientists and other kinds of scholars. They were, perhaps, absurd, and yet, I would argue, they had an element of truth to them. One person, at a reading I gave of the book, asked me whether it was a novel—a question I found very interesting.

You Can See that I'm a Jewish Humorist?

Being Jewish, I am (it almost comes naturally) like many Jews, a Jewish humorist. There is an enigma about Jewish humor. How come the Jewish people, who have suffered so much, have such an incredible sense of humor? "Why do you want to know?" would be a Jewish response, since Jews are supposed to always answer questions with questions. In my book *The Genius of the Jewish Joke* I explain that it has helped Jews survive—psychologically and physically—over the millennia.

It is my sense of humor that characterizes me and which has shaped my life and career, to a certain extent. I am, as I confessed earlier, an ironist and a trickster, and I see life as a comic. Maybe even absurd. (One of my colleagues, in a department I taught in many years ago, wrote an evaluation of me when I was being considered for promotion to a full professor that said, "we thought he was an absurdist, but then decided he was an absurdity." I thought it was a wonderful line.) A better line was the review of my book *The TV-Guided American*, published in 1975, which concluded "Berger is to the study of television what Idi Amin is to tourism in Uganda." The best line was reserved for the editor of a very respectable journal of economics. I had sent (as a gag) an article titled "The Berger Hypotty-thesis" in which I argued that the toilet training of our senators and congressmen explained why they voted the way they do on the budget. The letter the editor sent me ended with the line:

> The editors of this journal have concluded that your article, "The Berger Hypotty-thesis" is not publishable in this journal...or any we can possibly conceive of."

This former colleague of mine, who called me an absurdity, also told me that my books were unpublishable, even though I had published half a dozen books at the time. "You trick editors into publishing your work," he said. "Your books should never have been published." When I asked him how come he had never published anything, he told me "my work is *too good* to be published." And that's where we left it. I have continued to trick naïve and foolish editors and publish unpublishable books. And his career and that of his cronies in his department was characterized as doing scholarly work that was too good to be published. Actually, I don't think he ever did any scholarly work and I'd be surprised if he ever published anything more than perhaps a chapter from his dissertation. If that?

If you understand my orientation to the world and you realize that I don't take myself seriously (which is where some of the trouble comes from) you get a different perspective on my work—or much of it, I should say—than if you don't. It was Santayana who said "the universe is an equilibrium of idiocies," and I think he was right.

Many years ago, my good friend Irving Louis Horowitz called me an adolescent...or maybe he said I *act* like an adolescent. At the time, I was 60 or so. I took that remark as a compliment. Irving was one of the gullible editors (according to my colleague) that I've "fooled"—but only nine or ten times. I also edited a series of reprints of classic books in mass communication for him. He had a great sense of humor. As he wrote, once, in rejecting one of my manuscripts—"I may be crazy, Arthur...but I'm not *that* crazy!"

I was very fortunate to move, from a small social science department to the Broadcast & Electronic Communication Arts Department at San Francisco State University. (I taught at this institution from 1965 until 2003.) My colleagues in my new department were very receptive to my interest in humor and popular culture, and I dealt with humor in many of the courses I taught there. I even developed a course on writing situation comedies and taught it there for many years.

In the latter years of my career, I started writing comic mysteries in which I could satirize scholars and university life. I assuaged my hostility toward academics by murdering numerous professors, and, at the same time, taught my readers about some subject. After I wrote *Postmortem for a Postmodernist,* about postmodernism, I wrote *The Hamlet Case,* in which a crazed professor murders the editorial board of *Shakespeare Studies,* which he edits. He fears the board is going to name someone else as the editor, so he bumps them off—but not before each of them has offered a different interpretation of *Hamlet.*

Killing professors, even though it is only in works of fiction, is, I find, very therapeutic. In another book, *The Mass Comm Murders,* I have five professors, all media theorists, murder one another. I hope that students who read this book will learn a good deal about media theories while enjoying the pleasure of seeing professors, hated authority figures for many, bumped off by being poisoned, shot, stabbed, thrown out of windows and blown up.

Publishing Books is Aggravating.

Publishing books is often quite aggravating, for a variety of reasons. Copy-editors go over your manuscripts and ask millions of questions. When you've gone over the page proofs and taken care of the index, you find that there are frequently long delays at the printers. Sometimes your editors make all kinds of ridiculous suggestions, and they often send your manuscripts to professors who make other suggestions and really want you to rewrite the book the way they would have written it. Or who trash the book.

Here's a selection from a jointly written review of my *Mass Comm Murders* manuscript that shows what I'm talking about. I don't know the names of the authors of this review:

> As written we are hard-pressed to think of any courses for which this book would be value-added. It would confuse rather than clarify. In contrast, we think that the edited book that Haddley-Lassiter [a character in my mystery who strings together quoted passages from famous theorists in a proposal for a book] would be a good companion volume to any Mass Communication Theory text...we cannot think of a media and/or theory text that would be enhanced by being used with Murder Go Round [the original title for my book]."

The review then concluded that I should rewrite the book along lines the authors suggest and come up with a completely different book:

> Such a rewrite would require Berger to start over. As it is now, the narrative in no way elucidates theory—it's simply a fairly clever story with fragments of theory thrown in rather haphazardly.

Reading a manuscript review like this helps explain, I think, why I find knocking off professors so therapeutic. (The book was published and did quite well, incidentally.) I should point out that sometimes you get valuable suggestions from the reviewers to whom your editors send your manuscripts.

There's an ironic conclusion to this story. Shortly after I got the review, I was having a Dim Sum lunch in a Chinese restaurant on Clement Street in San Francisco with Mitch Allen, the president of AltaMira Press, and I told him about the letter. "Why don't you do a book about postmodernism that's like that Haddley-Lassiter material in your mystery?" he asked. "That's a good idea," I replied. So I agreed to edit a book to be called *The Portable Postmodernist.* I then told him I had an idea for doing a mystery about sociology. "No," he replied. "Sociological theory. You've done postmodern theory. Now do sociological theory. Deal with Durkheim and Weber and Marx and other important thinkers."

"Hmm," I said. "That sounds like a good idea. How about calling it 'Durkheim is Dead.' I like the ring of that." He agreed and I wrote that book but as a Sherlock Holmes mystery. So those nasty comments by my reviewers led to two books.

I used to write a good deal of comic verse since I like to play with words. The first week I was in Minneapolis, as a graduate student in American Studies, I went to a party full of professors from the English department. One of the professors was holding forth about how terrible some poet named John Silken was. I asked him, "are you trying to make a sow's ear out of Silken verse?" It was that question that established my reputation with the English department as something of a wit. And I ended up teaching a psychiatrist how to write comic poetry. It paid well and it was a lot of fun.

In my dissertation, I explained that the term "Shmoo" is a variation on the Yiddish term "Schmo" or "Schmuck." As I wrote: (1970:115) "The world "Schmoo" is quite probably a modification of the Jewish term *Schmo* or *Schmuck,* which means either "fool" ("booby," "nitwit,") or "penis." I continued my analysis on the next page (1970:116):

> The most intriguing thing about the Shmoo, as I see it, is that it is a phallic symbol, and I say this for a number of reasons. The drawing of the Shmoo looks like an erect penis coming from a gigantic scrotum which emerges between two legs. (We might think of it as a wildly reductionistic fantastic creature—man reduced to a penis.) Capp also says that "they multiplies wifout th' slightest encouragement," which brings to mind the reproductive function of the penis.

Several of the professors on my dissertation committee were amused by my Freudian perspective and others thought I was out of my mind. None of them knew Yiddish, of course.

I interrupted my graduate studies for a year in 1963. I won a Fulbright to Italy and ended up in Milan, to do some research on the popular Italian magazine press—magazines such as *Oggi* and *Epoca* that had huge circulations. I researched these publications and my article on these magazines was published in an Italian social science journal, *Il Mulino*. In my article, I expressed amazement at how a very small staff of journalists could publish a weekly that had a huge circulation. I described these magazines as being like dinosaurs—with gigantic bodies and a brain the size of a pea. One afternoon while listening to the radio, a newscaster mentioned an article by an American sociologist (me) who described Italian weekly magazines as dinosaurs. It seems the Italians were taken with my description of the Italian weeklies as being like dinosaurs.

I taught two courses in American Studies at the University of Milan. One day I asked my students a question. "Who's doing interesting work in Italy on media and popular culture?" They all gave me the same name—Umberto Eco. He taught at the University of Bologna but lived in Milan, so I called him and got to know him. We first met at the Galleria and had a long discussion. We talked about my work on comics and my interest in popular culture. In Italian, comics are called "fumetti," for the puffs of smoke in which the dialogue is placed. Eco was, it turns, very much interested in popular culture and, in particular, in comics. He had recently written (or maybe he was working on) an article on Superman—known in Italy as "The Nembo Kid," because the Italians didn't want to use the word "Superman" due to its connection with fascism. Through Eco, I got to know several journalists and scholars doing work on comics in Italy and went to various publishers who were putting out collections of comics. I remember one evening, Eco and a group of other writers came to my little apartment in Milan. One of them asked for some Scotch. "Sorry," I said, "I don't have Scotch. All I have is grappa." Grappa is a very proletarian drink, but it was better than nothing, so they drank Grappa.

What I did when I analyzed comics and other forms of popular culture was to use the standard techniques of literary and cultural analysis but apply them to what were then known as "sub-literary" texts. I used psychoanalytic theory, I used sociological theory, I used literary criticism methods, but I used them on *Li'l Abner*, a comic strip, not a novel. When I was doing my research on *Li'l Abner*, I noticed that there were countless articles on Henry James and almost nothing on *Li'l Abner*, which was read by millions of people each day, all over the world. I was greatly encouraged by the work the Italians were doing in popular culture and comics and felt it validated my work. When I returned from Italy, I finished my dissertation and graduated from the University of Minnesota in 1965. I got a job teaching at San Francisco State and remained there until I retired. I did spend a year teaching pop culture as a visiting professor at the Annenberg School for Communication at the University of Southern California in 1984. I taught a large class of some 200 students. While I was in Los Angeles, I invited Stan Lee, an old acquaintance of mine, to give a lecture and he was kind enough to do so. He was trying to get one of his comic book characters made into a movie and having trouble doing so.

On the Future of Laughter

I was to have the last laugh at my colleagues who ridiculed me, for my dissertation was accepted for publication and appeared in 1969 as *Li'l Abner: A Study in American Satire.* It was later reprinted (thanks to the good offices of Tom Inge) by the University Press of Mississippi in a series of reprints of significant works on popular culture. Also, an article I wrote about attitudes on authority in the Italian and American appeared in a distinguished social science journal, *Transaction* (now renamed *Society*) and I was to eventually have a long relationship with the editor of this journal, Irving Louis Horowitz, who I mentioned earlier.

Thoreau tells a story about a publisher of his who gave him 3,000 copies of a book of his that hadn't sold. Thoreau later told a friend, "*I have a library of 5,000 books, 3,000 of which I wrote.*" In this respect, I should point out that in addition to my 102 journals, I've published more than 75 books, so I can say that *I have written around 175 books, 100 of which are about myself.* Some might say all of them are about myself.

In recent years, especially with the publication of Bakhtin's works, scholars in literary fields and cultural studies have become increasingly aware of the importance of studying humor and there has been a growing amount of scholarly interest in the subject. Years ago, William Fry and I organized a humor study group, BAHA (Bay Area Humor Association) which met from time to time at San Francisco State. We had some distinguished scholars from Stanford, Berkeley and San Francisco State who attended the meetings. There are many journals devoted to the subject, both here and abroad, and when you think about the importance of humor in television, film, books and popular culture, it becomes obvious that humor is a matter that permeates our lives. If we humor scholars do not get the amount of recognition we deserve from the academic powers that be, who are doing "serious" work, at least we have more fun. Or we *should* have more fun!

I would say that my interest in humor didn't cause problems for me in my career. My colleagues in my department were very supportive of the work I was doing, and so were many colleagues in other departments. It was my sense of humor and that caused me problems. (Should it be *my* sense of humor or my *sense* of humor? I'm not sure.) My irreverence and insouciance, I suspect, rubbed many of our university administrators the wrong way. Not that they could do much about it. And I'm sure I irritated all those overly solemn deadly serious types whose work is too good to be published that populate so many academic departments—many of whom, I have reason to suspect, ended up reviewing my manuscripts. The secret is to have editors send your manuscripts to be reviewed by friends. And *real* friends, not people who will knife you in the back. That's happened to me or more than one occasion.

So, I've spent many years, gleefully knocking professors off various ways (axes, knives, defenestration, poison darts, bombs), though I continue to write books on media and popular culture. It seems that I'm having the last laugh…and if I'm not amusing anyone else, at least I'm amusing myself. I've laughed and I've lasted.

Bibliography of My Publications on Humor

Books on Humor

Li'l Abner: A Study in American Satire 1970. Twayne Publishers.
The Comic-Stripped American 1974. Walker & Co.
The TV-Guided American. 1975. Walker & Co.
An Anatomy of Humor 1993. Transaction Publishers.
Blind Men & Elephants: Perspectives on Humor 1995 Transaction Publishers.
The Genius of the Jewish Joke. 1997 Jason Aronson.
The Art of Comedy Writing. 1997 Transaction Publishers.
Jewish Jesters. 2001. Hampton Press.

Comic Mysteries

PostMortem for a Postmodernist. 1997. AltaMira Press.
The Hamlet Case. 2000. Xlibris.
Aristotle: Comedy. 2001. Xlibris.
The Mass-Comm Murders: Five Media Theorists Self-Destruct. 2002. Rowman & Littlefield.

Index

4

A

B

C